"*Listen to Your Work* is an excellent resource for young people in business or, for that matter, any type of work. Also, this book will help mentors, like myself, extend our influence with young people. You reinforce many of the things that mentors say to their mentorees. If they do listen (and read) they will be much better off for doing so."

— Marvin N. Schoenhals, Chairman
WSFS FINANCIAL CORPORATION
WILMINGTON, DELAWARE

"*Listen to Your Work* is an easy read—no stuffy language. Andrews' key ideas are presented with clarity and precision."

— J. Thomas May, Chairman and CEO
SIMMONS FIRST NATIONAL CORPORATION
PINE BLUFF, ARKANSAS

"I was really taken by *Listen to Your Work*. It is relevant, its author articulate, and it focuses upon the most important principles of business. The book cuts to the heart of what makes a company work… If I'd had this book during my career, I would have used it as a regular reference text and reread it often to continually reinforce the sound principles of the "right way" to conduct business."

— Gregory S. Campbell, Chairman
SENTIENT FLIGHT GROUP
WEYMOUTH, MASSACHUSETTS

T0094867

Listen
TO YOUR
Work

Job-Active Advice from
a Battle-Scarred Mentor

Collins Andrews

Parkhurst Brothers, Inc.

PUBLISHERS

Little Rock, Arkansas

© Collins Andrews 2009.
All rights reserved.
Published 2009 by Parkhurst Brothers, Inc., 415 North McKinley Street,
Suite 280-J, Little Rock, Arkansas 72205.

Library of Congress Control Number: 2008939558

ISBN 978-1-935166-01-6 1 1-935166-01-8
Printed in the United States of America.
The paper in this book meets the standards for longevity
and durability established by the ANSI.

Dedication

To Adam, Spencer, Daniel and
your friends—my target market.

Acknowledgements

A few years ago I was meeting with Lance McGonigal, an IT manager whom I had worked with for a number of years as a mentor. Lance and I were discussing some kind of significant career issue for him—he had a lot of them—and I was telling a story from a previous employer describing a situation similar to Lance's. Suddenly Lance stopped me and said, "You have to write some of this down. These stories you tell have been so helpful to me, I know they would be helpful to other people." My response was quick, "You are an idiot!"

But Lance was persistent. The more he talked, the more I thought he could very well be right. I was telling stories based on experience, a good bit of it trial and error. I frequently saw similar patterns of behavior in other companies that were helpful to him. Lance and I developed an outline based on many of our previous discussions, and this book was on the way.

As a result, I must first thank Lance McGonigal for his belief in me, my ability to tell stories, and the value of my experience. He has been supportive and a sounding board throughout the development of the book, and I appreciate it.

I would like to thank my editor, Roger Armbrust, for taking my idea of a book and turning it into a real one. But I also must acknowledge the editing work of Crystal Baker, Angie Stahl, and Matt Bradley, who worked with original manuscripts of my disjointed stream of consciousness to help shape my thoughts and suggest improvements.

Two former employers, Scott Ford and Jeff Fox, took the time to read an early version, offering additional suggestions for content as did my friend, business professor Don White and the Acxiom Business Book Club. These people went out of their way to help early in the project, and gave me much-needed encouragement.

These writings would not be a book without the belief and backing of my publishers, Ted Parkhurst and Drew Kelso. These guys believed my book was worthy of investment, and have helped turn it into a reality.

Finally, what makes a book like this possible is work experience, and the opportunity to learn that comes from working with dedicated employees who want to be successful. In that respect I would like to acknowledge and thank the employees of Systematics, Inc., Alltel Corporation, ESI Group and Acxiom Corporation who worked with me over the years. These companies and their employees offered a lifetime of opportunity to me, and I am grateful for their hard work and support. I believe I was always able to gain more from my work experience than I contributed.

Collins Andrews
September, 2008

Table of Contents

Introduction – Why You Should Read This Book

These days, I seem to spend an inordinate amount of time talking with others about their careers. Surely this is just another life stage. Old enough now, I pose no threat to up-and-comers. I have experienced enough success so people at least want to equal it. And I certainly like to share my practical knowledge with others, particularly when I get to talk! In other words, my relevant experience can help young, aspiring professionals. It must have helped a few, because I keep getting calls.

Recently, a former co-worker (laid off, wanting help finding a job) told me, "People like you are the best references." Honest statements like that make me want to help. If someone asks for my help, I want to do the best I can for them. After working over 35 years, I have begun to treasure that invested time, energy and emotion. That's why I'm thrilled to assist people in solving organizational and career problems, and see them accomplish their goals.

I've written this book to support the early careers of professional business people: those who intend to work for others as a livelihood, and to dedicate significant time, energy and emotion pursuing their working dream. I believe we develop the strongest, most successful careers in the first few years. Those all-important early years can bring much frustration (they certainly did to me) as you transfer from an academic perspective to the real world.

People and organizations rarely behave as expected. What we call experience really comes down to understanding what people are going to do and why. It's usually based on example. If I can provide support and direction to move others' careers more rapidly, help them overcome conflicts, or even provide a little peace of mind and clarity, then this becomes a worthwhile exercise for them and for me.

These same insights should also aid people considering a significant career change: new company, new industry, new discipline, new department, or new role. I have been fortunate to work in quite a few different situations over the years, and at multiple levels. I've found consistencies in organizational, group and individual behavior that are predictable, and make it possible to anticipate, understand and plan career behavior.

In developing this book, I have tried to assume the business mentor's role. Obviously I am not your personal mentor. We do not share the face-to-face, open communication necessary for a successful, individual mentoring relationship. But a good mentor does not give advice directly. He or she draws out the mentee's thinking with open-ended questions, relevant examples, patience, and an equalizing openness and vulnerability. In this writing, I have assumed that we have such a relationship. I have developed the stories and opinions as if we were engaged in conversation, and you were interested in my comments.

For that reason, you may want to approach the book using the chapters as stand-alone discussions about a particular business topic, and not necessarily read all of them at once. Even I would get tired of listening to me after a while! I have summarized each chapter, and hopefully that will provide a later reference when, in the course of your career, some of these issues become personal.

This is a story about being inside organizations, told from an inside-the-organization viewpoint. It is not a quick list of successful behaviors guaranteed to transform your life. I offer an enduring message about what's important, what you should pay attention to, and what you should ignore. It is, in effect *our* story: lessons learned from *my* working lifetime, which will apply to *your* working lifetime.

If you are contemplating that first job or making a change, and are concerned about what you are getting into—read this book. It may be just what you need, pointing you in the right direction, accelerating the learning that your career, like all careers, will require.

The payoff: an improvement in your job satisfaction and your own personal *bottom line*.

What is a Mentor?

The word "mentor" originates in Homer's Greek classic *The Odyssey*. Odysseus entrusts his friend Mentor with the education of Odysseus' son Telemachus. In today's business context, we commonly define "mentor" as an individual, usually older, always more experienced, who helps and guides another's development. The mentor does not guide for personal gain. Chip Bell, in the mentoring guidebook, *Managers as Mentors*, identifies a mentor as "…someone who helps someone else learn something that would have otherwise been learned less well." Bell considers the relationship dominance-free: "Mentors are not power figures."

Recognizing mentors' value, some companies have established formal programs pairing experienced managers and leaders with up-and-coming employees to accelerate the younger workers' business maturity. The theory behind this investment: Inherent company value exists in rapidly developing younger employees' leadership skills—enough value to fund the investment in training. My limited direct experience with these formal programs has found they often involved well-intentioned management development efforts, but fell by the wayside to cost controls in difficult times.

Relating the mentor experience to natural human development: I believe value comes from pairing young people with those in later life stages, expressly so veterans can share skills to benefit those less-knowledgeable. A deep personal satisfaction can come from these exchanges. It goes beyond company goals, actually expanding human understanding for both mentor and mentee.

Looking back, I recall two individuals who truly played the mentor's role for me, both early in my career. Still, I have continued to learn from fellow workers throughout my career. In fact, I think willingly observing behavior, being open to change, and expecting to grow from your business relationships can keep you both humble and sharp. From my point of view, a true mentor relationship exists only when the learner is willing to change, and the teacher genuinely cares about the student's development and well being. This concern must be real; you cannot fake it. It remains the one best indicator of true mentoring.

In my first job after undergraduate school, I worked as an ingot metallurgist for Alcoa, assigned to an aluminum reduction and casting facility in Badin, North Carolina. The second recent college graduate hired there in 30 years, I was somewhat of a novelty. I had an immediate rapport with my boss, Charlie Barger, an engineer in his 40's. Charlie went to great lengths to make sure I understood my assignments, obtained all the resources I needed, was exposed to management, and received all Alcoa's formal training.

He went deeper than just offering support. We spent many hours talking about how the company worked, who was important and who wasn't, how to really get things done, how to advance—frankly, how to do my new job. I could truly "feel" his concern for my success. I responded with more questions every day, and all the effort I could muster. At the time, I didn't realize Charlie had become my mentor; but today I see how he gave me a good start. He particularly taught me how to work well with other people in a complex, interpersonal business environment.

After graduate school, my tenure with Air Products and Chemicals, Inc. also provided an excellent learning opportunity. I traveled extensively; became an authority on certain types of steel-fabrication equipment; worked with sales, production, vendor relations, engineering, and even began supervision. I also met my next mentor, George Metterhauser. A crusty, old welding equipment manager—and big talker—with 40 years on the job, he not only seemed to like me, but proved determined to keep me from becoming a jerk! Or at least any more of a jerk.

George's language was crude, but he took time to explain the welding equipment industry, the competitors, Air Products' weaknesses (welding equipment was one) and what customers expected. Very direct, clear, and absolutely no nonsense, George had strong opinions. He classified our co-workers, describing who was strong and at what, who was a whiner, in over his head, all talk and no "do"—essentially who helped the company and who didn't.

Hard of hearing, George always used a speakerphone turned to full volume. He would let me sit in his office and listen unannounced to these calls. I learned more from this eavesdropping than any management class. These conversations appeared to be one of his favorite pastimes. My first exposure to business politics, I learned that workers' manipulation often had more impact on an organization than their individual job contributions. It also made me want George to consider me a good guy, not a jerk.

As I look back now, I realize both Charlie and George cared about me as a person, and wanted to see me succeed in both business and personal life. They got a thrill out of working with me. Not understanding these relationships, I just thought they were good guys. I owe them so much. They willingly took their personal time to make sure I received a good start. Now, I believe they benefited as much from our time together as I did.

I have since had the good fortune to become a Charlie and George to a few people. I've written this book with those working relationships in mind. I am telling you—a young business professional who I want to succeed—what to expect, what is important, and what you need to know. That is, if you are listening!

How Do I Get Started?

Throughout high school and my undergraduate college years, my view of work and a career involved simply having a "job". I expected this job to come from some company or organization that wanted me for my knowledge and skill; but I really had no clue. I had no concept of a career, and certainly not a career plan. Naïve and with no knowledge about planning ahead, I suddenly discovered my senior year in undergraduate school that I needed a job. Engineering students were in a fortunate position back then. With many companies hiring engineering graduates, on-campus recruiting proved active and productive. As students coached in the interviewing process, we received plenty of advance notice about companies coming on campus to hire graduates.

The year was 1968, a time of significant social upheaval (driven by my own baby-boom generation's move through adolescence) and the Vietnam conflict. After WWII and throughout the 1960s, males over age 17 were subject to the military draft. They'd be called into the armed services unless they received some kind of draft deferment. College, at the undergraduate level, ranked as the most common deferment; but in my 1968 graduate year, the only post-graduate educational deferments went to medical or divinity students.

However, technical employees were in demand. Engineers, in particular, could opt to work in jobs considered important for national defense (defined as critical-skills jobs) as an alternative to obtaining a draft deferment. I married my high-school sweetheart during my senior year, and planned simply to obtain a critical-skills job and start earning a living.

I decided to take advantage of on-campus interviewing. Because of my metallurgy specialization as a mechanical engineer, I looked at companies that manufactured metals, or used them extensively. Since I had worked for Reynolds Metals for two summers, I targeted a preference toward the aluminum industry. You measured an interview's initial success by whether or not the company invited you to make a plant trip—a visit to one of the company's factories, presumably where you would work. The more plant trips, the more successful the interview process. I received plant trips from Reynolds, Alcoa, Caterpillar and Hamilton Standard.

While I had some desire to attend graduate school in business, lack of an available draft deferment made that plan moot. I chose the position as an ingot plant metallurgist (trainee) with Alcoa in Badin. We moved to North Carolina the week after graduation, resulting from not much of a decision process. Caterpillar and Hamilton Standard were located up north, too far away. Reynolds sat too close to home in Arkansas. Alcoa thrived in the south, in an industry I was comfortable entering; and the available position showed high likelihood of a "critical skills" classification.

That was it. No review of company financials, no industry market research, no career-path investigation, no advancement plan, no benefits comparison. It was simply an engineering job that paid the best salary I had been offered (around $800/month). Compared to today's employment market for graduating seniors, it was a lucrative time and a great opportunity!

As I look back, I focused only on getting a job as an engineer and earning a living. My only reference for the right alternative consisted of my previous summer work experience and my school contacts. Now I see the limits of that perspective. I had no concept for measuring my own strengths and weaknesses, and no industry contacts to help me gain an unbiased perspective of what to expect or even look for.

I would have benefited from some guidance, now known as mentoring. For example, my Alcoa plant—located in a town of 10,000 people—had hired only one other student right out of college in 30 years. I took a quality-control position in a low-volume specialty plant set in a small town considered a retirement haven. While happy to have a job, I found myself in a no-growth area, and plant leadership having no idea of what to do with me. My wife and I burned up the road to Charlotte every weekend just to go shopping!

This job choice showed me negative elements of my personality and decision-making style that I have worked to overcome. Essentially, I am inclined to choose the safest, most familiar, least-conflict alternative rather than push myself to see what I can accomplish. In this case, I assumed I should become an engineer (although I had only limited knowledge of those skills and requirements) because I had some exposure to the industry. I took a no-brainer path of least resistance.

I might have happily settled into a routine with Alcoa. But my wife's dissatisfaction with the small town, and my observing minimal growth or leadership potential in quality control, created the energy that led me to seek alternatives. Time on the job and exposure to other training locations made it clear that, in Alcoa's aluminum production business, plant managers were king. Some young, aggressive hotshots in plant management jobs were described in almost reverent terms, and sure caused people to jump! I quickly decided that was the job I wanted, and began to make plans.

In undergraduate school, I determined the best alternative for establishing a good career: get a master of business administration degree (MBA). While I didn't exactly know what that meant, conventional wisdom among engineering students identified an MBA as the path to management. After a few months at Alcoa, I applied to Purdue University's Krannert School of Management in Indiana. Krannert accepted me into its one-year master's program in industrial administration—similar to business, and targeted to engineers and science majors. Two of my friends had attended the previous year, and thought it excellent preparation. I assumed they were right. They both got jobs with management potential upon graduation. Again I took the risk-free route, applying to this one school. I somewhat regret not considering many schools, including the top ones, but that's a minor lament. With management as a goal, I quit Alcoa and moved to Indiana.

At this point, I still saw large-factory jobs as my career. My view remained dominated by the engineering method of problem solving. I barely understood why these businesses existed, or what made them successful. I saw jobs, not businesses. That perspective changed in graduate school. The focus became business. Much of our out-of-class discussion centered on the best ways to make money. Making money became a priority. I guess because I needed more than I had; and all these smart fellow students and professors talked about it all the time.

Clearly, using that standard, jobs that paid more money ranked higher on our list. The amount of starting salary became the measure of a person's worth. I have always been competitive. Maybe because of my "be nice" southern background, you could call me a "closet competitor." I knew some of my fellow students, the ones I viewed as unapproachably smart, would end up with higher measures than me (starting salaries). But I expected to perform well above average, matching my self-image.

In graduate school, we concentrated on getting a job. We treated on-campus interviews with similar preparation and angst as final exams. In my case, my aluminum-industry experience proved a starting point for selecting companies to interview; I probably assumed this as my fallback alternative. I also interviewed with companies known to hire MBAs, quickly classifying them as responsible positions with commensurate higher starting salaries.

A good friend from Vanderbilt worked at one of these companies, Air Products and Chemicals, Inc. Able to help me secure the right interviews, he also guided me on what to say to whom. The firm offered a position starting at $1,200 per month. The actual job was a little vague. But Air Products operated a small welding-equipment division that seemed to involve metallurgy. That was good enough for me.

Through the interview process, I learned an MBA provides no direct path to management for large, capital-intensive companies such as Alcoa and Reynolds. Amazing, but those companies wouldn't consider turning a 24-year-old rookie loose to manage one of their multi-million dollar factories. Makes a lot of sense today, but it didn't then! I considered them unenlightened and not progressive. I was wrong, they were right.

My view today: College education alone will not prepare you for the challenges of company leadership positions. Never expect them to hire you because of what you know. Your college degree proves you can learn, and provides a general background to start working. Then you begin creating the knowledge that makes you truly employable—the knowledge you gain from job experience.

In the course of interviewing aluminum companies, I talked to a Carrollton, Georgia wire manufacturing firm, Southwire Corporation. I hit it off well with their representative, who invited me to their corporate headquarters for a second interview. They actually flew my wife and me both down to Georgia on a small plane. They proposed a position as assistant to their president, including opportunities to work with him on various projects as I learned the business. Carrollton was a small town similar to Badin. The starting salary came to about $900/month.

My eyes beheld only the salary, and I even tried to negotiate a higher paycheck. I remember how our discussion turned negative when I tried to push them for more money. They were probably testing my willingness to commit to the company, and not consider money my only motivator. I made the wrong decision. Air Products was, and is, an excellent company. But Southwire would have offered me high-level exposure in a sound business where I had some basic technical expertise. Money should have ranked lower at that time in my career.

In today's market, any job with career relevance and growth opportunity may prove worthwhile for a college graduate. You must understand: companies hire you for a skill set—characteristics and abilities to help you accomplish results benefiting your employer. You are NOT hired for what you have learned in school. In fact, outside of your immediate family, no one cares what you have learned, and they certainly do not want to hear about it.

You do not need to find the ideal company for your first job. In fact, you should approach your initial employment assuming two basic things: (1) you are there to do your best and learn, and (2) as long as you are gaining experience and knowledge, you will become a better employee. And that is a good position. It's truly hard to understand what your job situation will be until you actually work inside a company. If you make a good, long-term selection on your first try, consider it a miracle. Many people become disenchanted with their first position within a year or two. They begin to understand what work and companies are like, and what they personally consider acceptable. I believe people tend to find more satisfaction in subsequent positions and companies—not because the company is any better—but because their personal expectations change with an understanding of reality.

I remember much discussion, particularly in graduate school, about the pros and cons of small business. Certainly a strong element of support existed for small business. Proponents used the logic that, working there, you can obtain broader responsibility faster. They implied value in this broader responsibility: it allows you opportunity to function at a higher level and learn more. Since I have now garnered experience in both large and small companies, I have an opinion on this issue.

Historically, finding small-business positions has proved difficult because these companies cannot afford to recruit on a broad scale. Typically, they hire based on reference only. This situation has somewhat improved with today's technology. Small businesses now can advertise, use recruiters, and post jobs on the Internet just like the big boys. The search is more difficult, but with diligence, extensive networking and patience, you can find the opportunities.

It's probably true that you receive broad experience in small business, but don't assume that makes high-level responsibility easier to obtain. Broad responsibility also means more low-level responsibility, because someone has to perform all the little tasks as well. In a small business, you should expect to do more copying, running errands, packing, cleaning, filing, printing and many thousand other tasks required to function in a business. You will surely gain an appreciation of these tasks; and you will understand that the phrase "someone has to do it" refers to you. This can be rewarding as well. But do not go into a small business thinking that you will rise to the top quicker. Essentially, you will find that the people at the top also work at the bottom!

Many small businesses are also family-owned, or individually owned. That structure deserves some discussion. Early in your career, set your goal to find positions where you can learn as much as possible. That means exposure to the company's products and services, and to their traditional disciplines of sales, product creation, marketing, engineering, operations, manufacturing, and eventually management.

Since you invariably will start at a low level, it does not matter who owns the company.

I worked with Ben Pearson Manufacturing Co. to develop Metal Services, Inc. We started a small business from scratch, operating out of a modest rented facility, trying to spend as little new money as possible. I co-opted old Ben Pearson office furniture, and in the process came across the founder's terrific unused wooden desk. I commandeered that desk, with the company's blessing of course, and thought it was pretty cool. One day the Ben Pearson maintenance guys literally took the desk back, leaving me with an empty office! As it turned out, the owner's son was coming to work for the business, and he needed a desk. I read the sign: we take care of family first. While desks (and all office trappings) are really unimportant, the symbolism matters. It represents control and compensation issues within family-owned businesses.

As you develop a longer-term view, planning for your career's middle and later stages, you should become concerned with wealth building. Invariably, you best accomplish this through ownership participation. Do not be fooled by rhetoric. Blood is thicker than organization charts! Typically a family business's long-term goal involves preserving the family's wealth (ownership). Sharing ownership does not accomplish that preservation. Again, like many issues you'll deal with, this is not a matter of bad or good. It is just how business functions. Projecting another result will lead to disappointment.

Do not expect to make a quick hit, building wealth in a short period of time. Never make your employment decisions based on the opportunity for a home run. Such chances are rare. A better strategy: Look for companies that let you participate in ownership over time, and where your ownership value likely will grow. Think of this ownership accumulation over a 15- to 20-year horizon, not a five-year horizon.

You find the right job, first, by finding the right company; and by that I mean a good company. High on the list of company measurements: profitability. In particular, profitability demonstrated over time, through some kind of identifiable value of how the company makes money. I believe you should select companies that try to please their customers, and show open dedication to creating a good working environment for their employees. Most companies will say they do this well; but you can easily confirm it by talking to their customers and employees. If you experience roadblocks to having these conversations, there is probably a reason. In simple terms, successful companies are better employers. You should always seek opportunities with organizations offering you the potential of a long-term career.

In addition, be aware that you, and only you, are responsible for your career. You should select companies that offer training beyond on-the-job; but ultimately you set your goals, you achieve them, and you "own" your progress. Do not blame your company if they do not give you an opportunity. Rather, understand what you would like to accomplish. Realistically include that as part of your objectives, sharing it with your employer. If you cannot create reasonable objectives and work toward them with your employer, you should look for work elsewhere.

You can reasonably expect two or three different careers in a working lifetime. As your knowledge of business and, more importantly, of yourself matures, anticipate your perspective changing. This will manifest in ideas for new positions and new industries that you will be inspired to try.

This can be healthy. Don't be afraid to make significant job-role or industry changes if you have thoroughly thought them through, received supporting advice from people you trust, and have your family's support. Never make a job-change decision without thoughtful review. It's easy to allow job selection to become an emotional decision. It should never be. It is just business!

Now, let me tell you the most difficult challenge in my business career: My employment value inevitably matured, affecting my job roles. In my career's first 30 years, I never considered slowing down. I believed I could achieve any position if I put enough energy into it. After 20 years with Systematics/Alltel, I realized that my accomplishments, and their advancement rewards, had ended. I would not become the CEO.

Through good fortune of my long-term employment and ownership participation, I could consider retiring. I began to realize the pure enjoyment of working, as opposed to the competitive push for the next high position. I slowly began to realize again the thrill of being involved, contributing to a group, having people depend on me, and most of all, helping make other people's lives better. Over the last few years, this has become my career focus, and a true thrill! Playing a role in helping others achieve their goals, make more money, and contribute to society is the essence of work's value. And I get paid for this!

Our working lives involve a value cycle. It is virtually impossible to manage that cycle so it will increase continually until you retire. In other words, you will not be able to manage your career so that you always get promoted and advance, thus moving to your highest possible contribution/achievement level, culminating with retirement. Your value will not be that linear. That is not human nature, and you should not expect it in business.

On the other hand, the following expectation is perfectly acceptable, and desirable: Start your career with a willingness to learn, to advance, and to make more money. As you mature, your energy level, learning and physical abilities will all decline. In contrast, you will continually gain insight into your contributions, your knowledge, and what is important to you. Work to understand yourself, and set realistic goals for your skills, knowledge, and ability. Then you can expect your job satisfaction to remain high throughout your working life. If you are sincere in this effort, I've no doubt a mentor or two will appear along the way, helping you in this career process.

Chapter Summary:
- Never expect the knowledge gained in your education to be the reason a company hires you.
- Your education proves that you can learn, and provides you a general background to start creating the knowledge that makes you employable—knowledge you gain from job experience.
- It is not necessary to find the ideal company for your first job.

- You should approach your initial employment assuming that you are there to do your best and learn. As long as you gain experience and knowledge, making you a better employee, it is a good position.
- Do not think that working for a small business will get you to the top quicker. Essentially you will find that people at the top also work at the bottom.
- Early in your career, find positions where you can learn as much as possible by exposure to the company's products and services, and the traditional disciplines of sales, product creation, marketing, engineering, operations, manufacturing, and eventually management.
- The long-term goal of a family business is to preserve the family's wealth (ownership). Sharing the ownership does not accomplish that preservation.
- Do not expect to make a quick hit and build wealth in a short period of time.
- Never make your employment decisions based on the opportunity for a home run.
- Look for companies that provide ownership participation over time, and where your ownership value is likely to grow. Think of this ownership accumulation over a 15- to 20-year horizon, not a five-year horizon.
- Select companies that try to please their customers and show dedication to creating a good working environment for their employees.
- You, and only you, are responsible for your career.
- It is easy to let job selection become an emotional decision. It should never be. It is just business!
- All of us have a value cycle in our working lives. It is virtually impossible to manage that cycle so that it continually increases until retirement.

General Business – The Role of Money

Typical of young, technical people new to the job market, I understood very little of business until I garnered some specific training and experience. I knew what happened in manufacturing, understood supply and demand, and discerned what it was like to have a job. But I possessed no insight into the financial side of business, value creation, investment, or even why business existed. I understood the personal need for money, and the necessity to spend within your means. However, to me, obtaining money meant figuring out how to get it from those who had it! My view began to change when I entered a graduate business school.

In business school, money was the backdrop, part of every class's essential material, and clearly the measure of worth. In addition, my social network of students and professors implicitly appreciated small business and entrepreneurs. They revered people who had hit the big-money "home run" through their own initiative, and shared many stories about starting small businesses with lucrative returns. This small-business lure still somewhat mystifies me, but I believe it centers on controlling time and decision-making—in short, to regulate what you do and when you do it.

I have learned that such control is an illusion. There is always a boss. In all business you will answer to someone. You will always have more to do than time available to do it. Work is not always fun. It is hard, but can be immensely rewarding. While my primary graduate-school objective involved finding a job with a high starting salary, my network was sowing the seeds of small business. I began seeing my complete control of the business as an end game.

In my first post-grad-school job with Air Products and Chemicals, I became the product manager for a line of shape flame-cutting machines. It gave me the opportunity to work with sales, engineering, and more importantly, customers. The company theoretically measured my performance by product profitability; but this position typically involved staff support to the sales, engineering and manufacturing operations, with little decision-making authority. The profit responsibility was basically meaningless, because I had no authority to make any significant changes. But the position afforded an excellent training ground, inherently exposing me to how the machine was made and sold, and how it helped its users.

One customer, a small company named Specialty Manufacturing, was run by three young engineers. It used our flame-cutting equipment to serve manufacturers. The business model involved simple economies of scale; the expensive machine was hard to operate. These guys became experts at it, working this equipment at maximum throughput and efficiency. By providing flame cutting as a service, they could leverage the machine's value over a number of customers, profitably optimizing their equipment investment. With their help and support, I began formulating the idea of starting a similar business in a different geographic market.

Using case templates from marketing class and finance-class spreadsheets (this was years before PCs, Excel, and the Internet's small-business templates), I developed a business plan which seemed sound. Then I set out to find the start-up capital. Understand I was 25 years old, living in a new part of the country, with very few business contacts. I placed a blind ad in the *Wall Street Journal*, asking for new-business funding. I contacted a few state Chambers of Commerce, using people I knew (nowadays we call this networking) to meet a few bankers and investors. Looking back, I'm still amazed. I initiated conversations with two private investors serious enough to meet with me a few times.

I planned to use their money, build the business, and pay them back with a return. It made sense to me, but eventually not to them. For this small amount of money, I did not understand why they would not invest in this sure 20%+ return I offered. In fact, I found them both a little cold and insensitive when I asked for their decision. Eventually they wouldn't even return my phone calls! They apparently concluded that my ability to successfully implement and maintain this business created too great a risk for the projected return. I have since learned that money, through investment and return, is the heart of business. It's not a chicken and egg situation. No investment, no business, period. That's why the money source demands (and deserves) so much control in business. Money goes where it is appreciated through generating optimal returns.

In the course of all this talking, a bank submitted my business plan to Ben Pearson Manufacturing Company, a family-owned business in my hometown of Pine Bluff, Arkansas. A small farm-implement manufacturer, Ben Pearson was experiencing high demand for its product, a mechanical cotton picker. Some of the machine's key components required heat treating and chrome plating. The closest source for these services was located in St. Louis. As a result, they frequently encountered production delays due to logistics, and high costs due to shipping and the third parties' markup. Ben Pearson was interested in starting a business to provide these metalworking services, using the same "economies of scale" model as Specialty Manufacturing.

After considerable negotiation, we formed Metal Services, Inc., a small business providing heat-treating, chrome-plating, and flame-cutting services. Ben Pearson owned 80%, I owned 20%. Ben Pearson (not I personally) secured a bank loan for most of the start-up capital. I'm still pleased that I could start this business with little personal risk. But as I look back on other decisions, I can see we were likely doomed from the start. The services we chose to provide all depended on volume and shipping cost, so a few large customers and low shipping costs were a must.

Because I had been planning a flame-cutting service business, I insisted on adding equipment and services I had modeled from Specialty Manufacturing. This type of service, used in steel fabrication, made small manufacturing firms our primary market. At Ben Pearson's insistence, we located in Pine Bluff, a town with little manufacturing business and no interstate highway. We were located too far from our potential market. I had a gut feeling that we should have set up the business in Little Rock, somewhat a transportation hub and more of a metropolitan area. I was unwilling and unable to argue persuasively. We eventually faced serious price competition, a result of oversupply created by the mid-1970s energy crisis. Our bigger-city competitors ate our lunch.

The point: Ben Pearson supplied most of the start-up capital and bank guarantee, resulting in ownership and decision-making control. All through the business's start-up, they influenced decisions in ways that seemed to their advantage, but in the long run hurt our prospects. I proved complicit in the failure. I knew issues existed with location and availability of a market to serve; but I let my emotional desire to start the business supersede common sense.

Still, what a learning experience! I led strategy, business development, engineering, production, purchasing, construction, community relations, human resources, recruiting, quality control, drafting, building maintenance, customer service and a host of other jobs where I possessed suspect qualifications. I controlled many disciplines, but was never in control.

In retrospect, I should have altered my decision and never started this business. I lacked the knowledge and experience to understand the negative message knotting in my gut. Instead, I listened to my ego and emotions. The lesson here: ALWAYS listen to your intuition. If you suspect a problem, one usually exists. You just haven't defined it. Stop and take the time to rationally and systematically challenge your assumptions. *Write down* why you have a gut feel (positive or negative). If you can continue to proceed with that documented caution, then go for it!

When I quit working and semi-retired 25 years later, I saw this small-business investment picture from the other direction. Due to Systematics' business success, I had gained enough money to live on, affording to do what I wanted. I planned to rely on my experience, working as a consultant; at least working enough to pay for my downtown office, and possibly invest in small businesses, staying involved at a board level. After reviewing many new business plans and investment opportunities, I learned why start-up capital had proved hard to find for my own business. I now expected two things: (1) a return for any money I would invest, and (2) to remain in reasonable control over the money's use, or else I would not provide it! Most business ideas are bad, and many people want to spend other people's money.

Most thoughtful companies, large or small, will create a series of broad, strategic statements—guiding principles for their behavior. They will try to sum up their business in a few sentences, invariably including some platitudes related to customers, employees and money. Money may take the form of stakeholders, shareholders, investors, profit, growth, revenue or some combination of these. The firm's guidelines can prove helpful for leadership; some will argue they're even critical. More than likely, every word will be painstakingly reviewed, with statements crafted to reflect the company's unique culture and market. See Table 1 for a series of these statements, spanning 20 years, from companies where I have worked.

In each case, I could spend an hour passionately describing the role each statement played in our company, becoming guiding principles for most of our behavior. Notice their similarities, even though different in origin and time period. These important statements allow consistency in worker communication, and help management create focus and direction for the employees.

I believe today's employees should expect this kind of focused leadership communication. However, take care to treat these statements for what they are—similar across companies and designed to facilitate communication and to focus behavior—not for what they aren't: gospel. Business gospel is much simpler than that. Customers must be treated well and realize value; employees must be fairly compensated and motivated; and most of all, investment drives business and expects a return. You must never forget: this business "stuff" is all about money. Money remains our only real, universal measure of accomplishment. Consequently, investment leads the sequence of events that create and maintain business, and that investment demands a return. It doesn't matter whether investment comes from a group of individuals, a company, the public market, or one person. The anticipated result is always a return—e.g. growth, more than you started with. This basic principle is probably as old as civilization. We've certainly documented it throughout history, even

TABLE 1 – COMMON CORPORATE GUIDANCE STATEMENTS

Company Goals - Acxiom Corporation, 2005
• To create value for our associates by building a progressive work environment where we inspire, empower, challenge and recognize our people
• To create value for our clients by delivering a positive impact on their business results
• To create value for our shareholders by generating a significant return on their investment
Corporate Objectives - Systematics, 1994 (after acquisition by Alltel Corporation)
• Customer Objective – At Systematics, the customer always comes first. Our objective is to achieve complete customer satisfaction and to cultivate long-term business relationships through superior products and services and an abiding commitment to customer satisfaction.
• Employee Objective – Systematics has, from its inception, striven to employ the very best people available and provide them with opportunities for individual growth and success.
• Shareholder Objective – Systematics' commitment is to maximize shareholder value through continuing profit growth, without compromising our commitments to quality, to our customers and to our employees.
Corporate Objectives - Systematics, 1985
• Client Objective – To strive for complete client satisfaction by providing high quality products and services which meet the full range of financial data processing needs for all levels of our clients' personnel.
• Employee Objective – To employ the best people available and provide them with opportunities for personal success and satisfaction unequaled by others in our industry.
• Growth Objective – To increase total revenues and net income at the maximum rate consistent with maintaining high quality service and client satisfaction.
• Profit Objective – To achieve sufficient profits to provide a fair return on our shareholders' investment and to finance achievement of our other corporate objectives.

in the New Testament's parable of the "talents." (Apparently the Lord expects a return on investment, just like you do.)

Still, you must realize that, while money drives business, a business driven (or guided) only by money likely will fail. In other words, money represents the "why" of business, but cannot become the "what". A successful, growing, sustainable business rises from a complex combination of value creation and relationships. You must create something of leverageable value and someone must choose to buy it. The buyer must then remain satisfied with the product as well as the business relationship. Consequently, business leadership must artfully balance the interrelated interests of investors, customers and employees. Too much emphasis in one of these areas can be well intentioned, but fatal.

I have some direct experience here. The three successful companies where I played an executive role—Systematics, Alltel and Acxiom—approached this balance differently. All three successful companies used vision and purpose statements to describe their beliefs, emphasizing customers', employees' and shareholders' roles with rhetoric that sounded identical. It would certainly have been interchangeable.

But the companies had formed distinct personalities: Systematics placed a primary interest in its customers, Alltel in financial performance, and Acxiom in employee satisfaction. In each case, I believe the company personality evolved directly from the CEO, around his business beliefs and behavior. These companies will argue that they maintained a proper balance between these interests—the three-legged stool. Inside them, however, the contrasts were clear. They each behaved differently, emphasizing the primary focus in most of their leadership behavior. All three approaches worked. So we learn that no one approach is sacred. What matters are consistency, focus, and balance.

I hate to admit it, but I have come to believe that the best businesses are led by slightly unreasonable demands. Since I think like an engineer, I want business to be logical, sequential, and orderly. But like most of life, it is not. I have observed that people must receive some kind of push to perform at their best. The push may come internally (I admire those people greatly) or, more frequently, externally, e.g. customers, deadlines, goals, targets, money, praise, management, and, of course, spouses. This same push, whatever the source, drives the growth that capitalism rewards.

Of course, a business's natural push occurs between employees and supervisors, but I have seen this push often between organizational disciplines such as sales and production, or sales and engineering. Frequently, to meet targets and get paid, sales organizations will push the limits set by the production and delivery disciplines. If the corporate goal is maximum growth, expect sales or management to be the drivers, requiring a push beyond what seems safe and reasonable. If the goal is short-term profit, expect the driver to be cost control, often implemented by raising the organizational level of spending authority, and tightening up the amount of centralized control.

Put in simple terms, never expect your organization (or department, business unit, division, team) to independently define and accept the kind of pressure it takes to grow. Expect that pressure to come from outside. This creates the tension and focus on results necessary for top performance and rewards from investors. While uncomfortable, it should be considered normal for successful business. The art here—and art abounds in business—is managing so the push remains reasonable enough to promote positive results.

Risk stands out as a current term for financial push. Phrases such as, "You have to be willing to take a risk," or "That is just a risk of business," are common. In most organizations, they really mean, "If this fails, you lose!" Intelligent, calculated business risks rarely occur. I'm referring to situations where pros and cons are thoughtfully developed, and all parties involved understand and accept the positive and negative consequences. More often, people who take risks and win receive rewards and temporary adoration; those that fail are abandoned. In my experience, the phrase "take a risk" just seems like a popular way to say, "Good luck!" Risks fail more from poor planning than from bad people.

Pressure most often reveals an organization's or person's true nature. How people react to stress, crisis, hardship, or heartache tells more than hours of rhetoric. We naturally admire and respect (and want to be around) those who handle these pressures well. I like the term *grace* in this context. I think of people who handle pressure calmly—yet effectively—with logic, order, and concern for others and their surroundings as reacting with grace. You know people like that, and I bet you hope you have similar qualities.

Organizations are the same way. They must deal with pressure as an everyday occurrence. Invariably, we associate organizational pressure and stress with customer, employee, or financial issues; but, far and away, the one having the most effect on organizational behavior is financial. Lack of earnings, fiscal growth, or even not achieving forecasted financial targets will generate considerable stress and, in my observation, the most demonstrable and dramatic organizational reaction. The potential negative effect on investors and its resultant consequences sit at the heart of this reaction. We measure investor displeasure (any investor) via decline in stock price, demand for return of investment, or even the decision to "pull the plug" and quit the business. All of these measures pose serious threats to senior management's survival, hence the driving force behind organizational reaction.

I have received intimate exposure to organizational decision-making for cost-control purposes, including spending slowdowns, freezes, reductions and a number of significant layoffs. My first experience came with Systematics in 1987, when the founding CEO agreed to return to stimulate growth. From what I know now, he observed a typical pattern: excessive spending not directly associated with revenue. In other words, we had too many employees. Well intentioned, they performed professionally, but weren't necessarily generating or supporting revenue.

The CEO led a series of closed-door meetings with a select group of the executive staff. We reviewed all management personnel, one by one, starting with the list of employees in the top 5% of annual compensation. Our measurements were crude (they usually are), but we set a targeted expense reduction that quickly translated into a headcount reduction. We focused on people who, in our opinion, had risen to levels where their salary exceeded their contribution.

The point: These decisions were not scientific, but subjective, based first on hitting our targeted reduction in the company's compensation expense. We then considered what was legal, justifiable and defensible, and would cause the least company damage. Using a time-honored business theory about handling difficult work—when you eat shit, take big bites—we made all personnel cuts in one day (hereafter referred to as Black Monday). Once you make such decisions, popular management theory would indicate it's best to execute (no pun intended) quickly. The driving business reason for speed: to realize the savings' results; but it's just as important to minimize the length of disruption. We tried to be fair in paying severance and providing counseling and job placement services. But we were firing our friends, while knowing our own management failure caused these actions.

Another typical step in the cost management cycle involves raising the spending authorization level. Many businesses today operate under structures that encourage decision-making at the lowest organizational level possible. I believe this is the best organizational approach. It places spending control as close to the need as possible, and where knowledge is highest—an excellent way to develop positive managerial behavior with a large number of employees. When the business's goal is to significantly limit spending, however, this organizational structure becomes hard to control and may not restrict spending sufficiently.

Therefore, in a financial crisis, the organization typically will change its spending rules, taking authority away from many employees, and assigning it to a few higher-level executives. As an example, if you were a mid-level manager with a budgetary spending limit of $50,000 per item, that might be taken away. Then you might have to obtain approval from an executive (typically operational or financial, or both) for any spending above $5,000. I've made up these numbers, but the approach is common. This same process might also apply to hiring authority: where you once made hiring decisions, that power might be transferred to a senior executive.

This type of change definitely works, and represents a common short-term fix to dramatically reduce spending. I suppose it works because people typically become more careful and conservative when they must ask permission rather than make decisions on their own.

It's easier to justify something to yourself than to someone trying to avoid spending money.

The method's success may justifiably imply that management often distributes organizational spending authority at too low a level, and the only way to maintain proper control is to limit by centralization. In my experience, this is effective as a short-term fix only. Centralizing and tightly controlling decision-making authority eventually demoralizes developing leaders. It also causes employees to abdicate their responsibilities for good business decision-making. Employees will get on board, changing behavior to help save the business; but if the behavior change makes functioning at their jobs impossible, or causes them to feel undervalued, they will eventually resist, shut down, or leave.

The solution, like so many associated with business problems, involves constant, thorough and effective communications. If employees understand their actions' consequences to the overall business, not just to their individual areas, they can and should be held accountable to make decisions in the company's best interests.

I have played a similar role in at least six major cost-cutting initiatives since the first one at Systematics, all including major layoffs, and all performed in a similar manner. All, I might add, in some way resulted from management's failure to control expenses in line with revenue to respond to investors' growth demand. In every case, I was part of management, and in some way part of the problem. Today, companies are more efficient and sophisticated. They use more clearly defined guidelines to determine who is affected, and to provide counseling and job placement support to ex-employees. In fact, much of corporate America has become quite skilled at managing the layoff process. But the work and its consequences remain the same; good people lose their jobs, uprooting and devastating families and lives. Still, it is just business, and these necessary actions protect the company and the people who remain.

Organizations will go to great lengths to prevent these consequences, beginning with pressure to increase revenue (usually associated with additional risk), then moving to cost control, and finally to cost cutting. In most firms, salaries create a major expense, are a variable under management's control, and become the obvious target to control or reduce expenses. Over the last 15 years, American business has experienced an unprecedented increase in productivity, measured primarily by revenue per employee. For the most part, this dramatic change has occurred due to cost control targeted to improve financial performance; and the target for change has become the workforce. It's not that hundreds of companies simultaneously decided at the strategic level to increase productivity. The continuing investment demand for return forced management to pull the only levers available, and number of employees represents the biggest one. This is not bad; it is just the nature of business. However, if a firm has become lax in its controls, then strategic execution can become painful and damaging to all involved.

In summary, it has taken me years to learn and truly understand what may be obvious to others—business is all about money. At its basic measure, the origin of business depends on investment; its purpose is return on investment, and management must preserve that return for a company to survive. This is not bad or good; it is just how business works. Although managing business invariably leads to decisions significantly impacting individuals, executives make these decisions for financial reasons, not personal ones. This is the substance behind the saying, *"It ain't personal, it's just business!"*

Chapter Summary:

- Control is an illusion. There is always a boss. In all business you will answer to someone.
- Money, through investment and return, remains the heart of business.
- No investment, no business, period! That is why the source of money demands (and deserves) so much business control. It is also why money goes where it is appreciated.
- ALWAYS listen to your intuition. If you suspect a problem exists, it usually does.

- One of business leadership's primary tasks involves artfully balancing the interrelated interests of investors, customers and employees. Too much emphasis in one area, though well intentioned, can become fatal.
- The best businesses succeed due to slightly unreasonable demands!
- Never expect your organization (or department, business unit, division, team) to independently define and accept the pressure it takes to grow. Expect that pressure to come from outside.
- Intelligent, calculated business risks rarely occur. More often, people who take risks and win receive rewards and temporary adoration; those who fail are abandoned.
- Pressure most often reveals an organization's or person's true nature.
- Organizational pressure and stress result from customer, employee, or financial issues; but far and away, the one most affecting organizational behavior is financial.
- If employees understand their actions' consequences on the overall business, not just to their individual areas, they can and should be held accountable to make decisions in the company's best interests.
- Most layoffs in some way result from management's failure to control expenses in line with revenue to respond to investors' growth demand.

General Business – The Role of Customers

Customers play a leadership role in business. Don't kid yourself about your own value—"We work for the customer." "The customer is always right." "We are an extension of the customers' organization." "Our customers' success is our success." These and hundreds of other similar phrases accurately capture customers' value and, as such, successful companies' beliefs and behavior. In the long run, customers decide what they want, how much they will pay for it, what it is worth, whether they are satisfied, and whether we who serve them are successful. They pay our salaries and deserve our respect.

My customer perspective remains heavily influenced by my experience in technology-oriented service businesses, sold business to business, where long term agreements and relationships are the norm. It has become painfully obvious that successful products and services are those that customers need, and that provide measurable value. Unless we thoroughly understand our customers' business, we can't develop or deliver this kind of value. In other words, someone in our business must intimately understand their business. This knowledge cannot be superficial. We must relate to the issues our customers live with. That way, we earn their trust, and they favor us with their business.

My first exposure to this concept came as product manager with Air Products for its line of shape flame-cutting machines. Our product, of average capability, frequently had electronic breakdowns. In manufacturing, machinery breakdowns usually mean lost production—serious problems that demand prompt attention. As product manager, I was the corporate representative called in to help sell, or defend, this product. A sales representative brought me in to discuss frequent cutting-machine breakdowns with a small steel fabricating shop's owner. His company had not followed our maintenance guidelines. I was supposed to tell him that, if they would follow the correct procedure, they would not have these breakdowns. I do not remember how I worded this great advice, but I will never forget the owner's reaction. A big guy, he stood up, leaned over his desk and shouted, "The problem is you do not understand this business!" I wanted to hit him, and also disappear at the same time. I think we lost that customer eventually, but I can feel that guy's emotion today. This situation meant everything to him that day, and I wasn't helping because I wasn't listening.

Systematics used computing technology to deliver operational services to banks. I began working there with no knowledge of computer services or banking. After a few weeks of orientation and programming training, I received my first project: documentation for a new commercial loan system. Documentation was the lowest of jobs. No one wanted to do it, but it turned into an excellent learning assignment.

I developed a thorough knowledge of the commercial loan system by documenting its file layout and reports. This led to participating on the team for this system's second implementation. After that eventually successful effort, I was then a commercial loan "expert." I began presenting the system in sales situations, and helping on conversions. I was interested in commercial lending, which is creative, difficult to standardize, and the key to making money in most commercial banks. I enjoyed the challenge of adapting this system to client situations and working with commercial lending officers, relatively powerful people in banking hierarchy. With my sincere interest, I found the process fascinating.

The lesson here: It did not take much to become a Systematics commercial loans expert (evidenced by the fact that I became one while not knowing anything). The customers desperately wanted someone who could relate to them, was interested in their problems, and wanted to help.

I carried this approach further a few years later in Wichita, using my banking contacts to gain acceptance to Rutgers University's Stonier Graduate School of Banking. At that time, few IT employees were allowed in this prestigious school, which accepted only bank employees. I applied as if I was our banking client's employee, received the endorsement of our client's CEO, and became Stonier's first Systematics graduate. This school trains banking personnel to become senior executives. It exposed me to banking's core issues, significantly improving my ability to communicate with our senior-level clients. Just this small amount of attention to our customers' business allowed me, a Systematics representative, to gain acceptance with banking executives. It improved their perception of how we understood their business, and therefore our level of service.

Customers respect your commitment to understand their business, even if your knowledge falls short of theirs. However, a sincere desire should drive your effort to understand, and then help them. Superficial interest is obvious, and customers detest it. I have found them willing to share their business knowledge when asked, as long as my request didn't appear motivated by a short-term desire to get something from them. In the long run, both customer and supplier gain from common understanding, and customers almost always appreciate your sincere desire to help.

Lacking knowledge of a customer's business—this stands out as the most common deficiency among information technology professionals, whether they are working in-house or with outside suppliers. IT pros can be intelligent, hard-working, creative, and thorough; but their inherent focus on black-and-white solutions, and their love of technology, frequently remains out of touch with business reality. Technologists may create sophisticated and elegant solutions; but they frequently do not solve business problems, and are therefore not worth their expense. Inside Systematics, we frequently used a great phrase—which I attribute to founding CEO Walter Smiley—to describe this issue: "a solution in search of a problem." The IT world is overloaded with solutions in search of problems.

I have yet to see a business where good relationships with customers are not critical. A good customer relationship includes knowledge of your product or service, responsiveness, consistency, business understanding, communication skill, predictability and, of course, value. But in the end, it is all about trust. Is the customer confident in your ability to do what you say you can do? Can the customer count on your company to do whatever is necessary to help, or to fix problems when they occur? Can the customer *trust* you? Go out of your way to be precise and truthful, and the customer will reward you with trust and respect.

This is a serious subject. Being nice and offering entertainment does not create good customer relationships. With Pontiac State Bank as a Systematics client, we converted the bank's checking and item handling systems to new and relatively untested Systematics offerings. Despite the best efforts of our local staff and some imported Systematics experts, we developed serious problems during the item-processing conversion; the bank was unable to process its checks for three days. A bank's inability to process items for a number of days creates a grave problem, with the ultimate potential for significant losses.

Following those three problematic days, Ed Barker, the bank's crusty, no-nonsense CEO, visited me at 7:30 in the morning. When he walked in my office, I began explaining how we had the problem under control, using my typical friendly southern style. He cut me off, snapping, "Wipe that smile off your face and get us back in business!" He scared me.

Actually, we did have the problems resolved, soon processing and able to catch up on the weekend. But I must have acted in a way that Ed did not perceive as serious, or focused on his problem. He fixed my behavior right quick! In this case, we had expended the effort, and our people were on target; but I did not convey the understanding he expected. He could not trust me.

Customers are real people, with individual interests and abilities, as well as varying levels of responsibility. When dealing with an organization as a supplier, you *must* understand the roles and responsibilities of the people you work with. Then you know not only what to do for them, but also what to expect from them.

I classify customers as one of the following:

1. Users — Those people who deal with your company on a day-to-day basis, and obtain immediate value from your products and services. In many cases, these people are lower in the hierarchy. Their view of you relates only to how you impact them…today.

2. Influencers — While not decision-makers, these people influence decision-makers. They deserve additional attention; but they can be at any level, and unfortunately are sometimes hard to find. Good customer relationships include a deliberate effort to discover the influencers, and work to satisfy their needs.

3. Decision-makers — Obviously the most important customers, these people have the power and authority to kick you out and also to allow you to maintain your supplier's position. You should always know who they are, what they think, what they need, and how to improve your relationship with them.

This categorization may seem to be sales-oriented logic, but it can prove useful in all client relations. You should treat all customers with respect, just as you want to be treated. However, you must always be aware of how your and your company's actions impact those with significant influence on your ability to stay. In other words, like a politician, one of your primary objectives through client relations is to remain "in office."

In a service business, everyone has sales responsibility, and everyone is selling all the time. Sometimes, all you are selling is yourself; but you must always be aware that you are allowed to provide a service at the customer's will. When the customer loses that will, you are out of there, and likely out of a job.

Here's another difficult concept for IT professionals to grasp: customers define their own value. Clients clarify this by what they will buy, how much they will pay, and their commitment to remaining a customer. Cost has nothing to do with price, and technological sophistication is irrelevant unless it creates value. In countless meetings I have attended to define pricing for proposals and contractual relationships, the primary determinant for our pricing concept was our own costs. These sessions would be followed by mad scrambling to re-price when we realized the customer's payment limits.

Now, here's my favorite question for customers: "What problem are you trying to solve?" I have found that, if I ask that question and then keep quiet (very hard for me to do), the following discussion can be revealing and help build a relationship. Many times, customers will first present problems that are actually symptoms. Further discussion with people at different levels helps me understand the problem well enough to propose a solution. Time spent with customers in this manner (face to face is preferred) builds understanding and familiarity, leading to trust.

To me, trying to obtain and retain customers remains the most important part of a business's operational leadership. While investors provide the funding to initiate business activity, customers provide the funding to sustain it. Simply put, without customers there is no money.

Chapter Summary:

- Customers decide what they want, how much they will pay for it, what it is worth, whether they are satisfied, and whether those of us who serve them succeed. They pay our salaries, and we should respect them.
- Unless we thoroughly understand our customers' business, we cannot develop or deliver value. In other words, someone in our business must possess intimate knowledge of their business.
- Customers respect your commitment to understand their business, even if your knowledge falls short of theirs. However, a sincere desire should drive your effort to understand, and then help them. Superficial interest is obvious, and customers detest it.
- Technologists may create sophisticated and elegant solutions, but they frequently do not solve business problems and are therefore not worth their expense. The IT world is overloaded with solutions in search of problems.
- A good customer relationship includes knowledge of your product or service, responsiveness, consistency, business understanding, communication skill, predictability and, of course, value; but in the end, it is all about trust.
- You earn trust by always delivering on your commitments, understanding your customers' problems, and providing solutions that work. Always, always be honest. Never lie to customers. They always find out!

- You should treat all customers with respect, just as you want to be treated. However, you must always be aware of how your and your company's actions impact those who significantly influence your ability to stay. In other words, like a politician, one of your primary objectives through client relations is to remain "in office."
- In a service business, everyone has sales responsibility, and everyone is selling all the time.
- Customers define their own value. Cost has nothing to do with price, and technological sophistication is irrelevant unless it creates value.

General Business – The Role of Employees

Through my job roles, I have probably spent more hours working on employee-related issues than any other single task. Unfortunately, much of that time proved unproductive for my employers because it made them no money. I don't mean to imply that I wasted this time. Frequently it was personally rewarding; but conversations about employees do not generate income or satisfy customers, so they don't directly contribute to a company's worth. My fellow executives and I also spent endless hours talking about organizational structure, who should report to whom, how to motivate and measure employees, who should have responsibility for what—overall, how can we make the company better by "messing" with the employees or how they fit together. No doubt, employees make their companies great. But, over the years, much of what I have seen, and unfortunately fostered, I'd classify as tinkering, not improving.

Nothing is more important to a company's growth and well being than having the right employees. But when a company is fortunate enough to have them, nothing can prove less productive than trying to manipulate or motivate them through organizational structure, policy, and procedure. I believe you win the business game by focusing outside—on markets, needs, trends, competition, and most of all customers and prospects. Internal focus is never a winning strategy.

All companies possess a set of basic disciplines. In large companies, these disciplines are huge organizations in themselves. In small firms, they may be one person's overlapping responsibilities, but they exist just the same. The common disciplines include sales, product or service delivery (frequently called operations), engineering, information technology, product or service creation, marketing, accounting, human resources, and legal. "Executive management" fits together and theoretically controls these disciplines. "Senior management" individually controls them. These necessary areas make a company function, and lead workers to engage in predictable, common behaviors.

Sales employees are responsible for generating revenue. Most often, sales people are measured by the amount of new revenue, and are almost always directly compensated by the amount of money they generate. In simple terms, if they produce sales, they get paid. If they fail to produce sales, they do not get paid. Typically, management accomplishes this with low salaries (fixed compensation) and relatively high commissions and bonuses (variable compensation). Much of their compensation is at risk.

This type of payment system creates a natural set of behaviors focused around what they must do to get paid, and to minimize obstacles in that process. I have found that good sales people are not only comfortable, but also actually motivated by large variable compensation. When they are successful, they tend to make more money than employees in most other disciplines, and lose their jobs quicker when they fail.

Operations employees create the product or deliver services to customers; or, in more current language, they generate the value that customers purchase. These workers are measured by volume, timeliness, quality, and in the end, customer satisfaction. They tend to be short-term focused, intense, risk averse, responsive, and dedicated to getting the work out the door. Good operations employees will go to great lengths to assure their responsibilities are clear, and to instill trust in their relationships with customers. Their greatest fear: not getting the job done. The nature of their responsibility forces them to be precise and thorough as a way to avoid blame. Their compensation tends to be based on a higher fixed component than sales employees. The variable portion is based on obtaining or exceeding volume, timing or quality objectives.

Sales and operations are "line" positions, meaning they are directly responsible for generating company profits. Senior management typically controls them as individual silos; they are under the same executive only at the company's highest level. They have different missions, measurements, compensation, behaviors, personalities and temperaments; therefore operations and sales departments frequently experience internal conflicts. These are natural and normal conflicts, called "points of instability" by Walter Smiley. All organizations have these points of instability, and learning to anticipate and plan for their impact is part of gaining business experience.

As opposed to a firm's line functions, staff disciplines perform services supporting the line organization. Staff groups do not generate revenue, typically don't form customer relationships, and are not measured by profit. They are considered overhead, although they perform important services critical to any organization's success.

Who do I consider the most important of staff performers? The people dedicated to creating, or inventing, the products and services. In most businesses, these are the engineers. Engineers do not decide what to create, but rather how to create it. Their expertise is diverse, e.g. civil engineers in construction; mechanical and electrical in manufacturing; metallurgists in the primary metals industries; software engineers in information technology, and scores of other disciplines uniquely targeted to industry. Engineers learn the discipline to define and resolve problems; they tend to be analytical, thorough, focused, and in the best performers, creative. On the negative side, and painting their characteristics with a broad brush, engineers are brief and literal communicators (in other words, poor) who interpret in black and white. No shades of grey for this bunch.

Marketing is a staff discipline often confused with sales. Marketing provides supportive communication to customers and potential customers, and the line organization regarding a company's products and services. Marketing is not responsible for direct sales; it is more typically associated with promotional materials, branding, name recognition, advertising, and in the more sophisticated iterations, product and service strategy. To unfairly generalize, marketing people are typically good communicators, creative, and capable of abstract thought. Management does not measure them by immediate results such as direct sales or profit, so they tend to be less focused and driven than operational or sales employees. When viewed from inside the line organization, marketing people can appear somewhat out of touch with the important issues. From outside the line, they are likely viewed as broad, high-level thinkers.

Accounting represents another key staff discipline. These people are responsible for measuring the business's performance and ensuring accurate financial reporting within accounting standards. Before graduate school, I thought of accountants and their discipline as math, with right and wrong answers and only one correct method to produce results. I have since learned that accounting is a creative profession, with many ways to legally and correctly present financial information. Because their reporting measures success or failure, accountants are typically close to executive management and knowledgeable of business results. Good accountants develop an understanding and appreciation of the company, and become key management allies in leadership. Their proximity to executive management—and their need to understand and interpret business issues—make their communication skills a critical attribute. Accountants who are good communicators can become CEOs.

I see human resources' (HR) responsibilities in both offensive and defensive terms. The classic HR mission is defensive: understanding and implementing legally correct and effective employment policies. These include compensation, benefits, federal and state regulatory requirements, recruiting, hiring, dismissal and all employee-related activities. This segment is essentially designed to protect the company from wrongdoing and subsequent liability. In addition, some companies expand human resource responsibilities to include employee satisfaction, and development-centered activities such as market-competitive compensation and benefits, evaluation systems, satisfaction measurement systems, training, rewards, and community services. With these responsibilities, HR goes under the alias of organizational development (OD). I assume this is because of HR's typically defensive nature, desiring to concentrate on employment's positive side. Companies in tight employment markets—valuing their employees' improving contribution—are more likely to implement a formalized OD discipline. I see this segmentation as positive for employees. Companies with a well-developed OD discipline are usually good employers.

You will frequently hear the platitudes, "Our employees are our most important asset!" or "Our employees are what set us apart!" or some similar comment. These statements are true for most all companies. Employees *are* important. It is difficult to have a company without them.

Whether *you* will be an important employee is another story. Over the years, I have found that all employees are expendable. Of course, some are more critical than others, but even the most important worker can be replaced and the company will survive. This applies to each of us, as well as our bosses and co-workers.

In addition, it's rare for the assembly of individuals to make a company truly unique. For the most part, employees want to do a good job, contribute in a meaningful way, want their company to become competitive and successful, and to feel good about all this. Appealing to these desires creates an effective leadership approach. It can contribute significantly to motivational development, enabling hard work to occur over a long time period.

But you must realize it is not just the employees. Workable strategies, sound business models, sufficient investment, competitive offerings, attractive markets, and dedicated leadership all go hand in hand with the hard work and good people. This is what it takes to build a successful business.

A key factor for successful individual business performance is your ability to separate personal issues from business issues. Through our upbringing, families, education, and other group relationships, we have developed friends, relatives, competitors, allies, and even enemies. We know who we want to run with, and who we don't. We think we know how to get along, relate to others, be friends, team members, and contribute to society. I submit that business is a society unto itself. While work may seem like the other societies we know in our school, church, families, and common interest groups, it is not.

We must learn the principles of interpersonal behavior in business just like the rest of life. If we behave poorly, we will suffer, as will our business. This is hard because it all seems so familiar. We most often complicate and confuse this regarding our friendships. I believe you must distinguish between personal friends and business associates. Business acquaintances and co-workers are not friends. It is okay to be friendly with them; in fact, it is desirable. But do not make the mistake of assuming these individuals are friends.

To complicate it even more, you can develop working relationships with friends, but you must learn to separate "friend" behavior from work. In the end, we work to generate returns for investors, nothing more or less. Sometimes, accomplishing this requires actions not in the best personal interest of employees; but we have to take the actions. This can be minor, such as requiring people to work when they would rather not, e.g. on the weekend or during a vacation. Or it can be major, by laying them off or firing them. These are hard decisions you must make for the good of the company, and personal relationships make them all the more difficult.

After three years of working with Systematics in Wichita, I was promoted from account manager to district manager. In this new capacity, I became responsible for three account managers, two of whom also lived in Wichita. One of these (not my replacement) was my neighbor. He lived one block away and our children were friends. Until I assumed this new role, I knew the guy socially, but had little exposure to him as a manager. He seemed a little self-important, talking authoritatively about subjects he knew little about, but I did not think much of it. When I moved over to become his boss, I quickly saw that neither his client nor his employees respected him. In fact, some of our project failures led the client to question Systematics' capabilities; but I could see this was a leadership problem.

After concluding that a management change was necessary, I developed a plan to replace him. I selected a successor, negotiated his deal, put together a fair severance package, coordinated the change with the impacted clients, and built up my courage to hold the conversation with my neighbor. This took a few weeks to plan. About a week before this final conversation, I told my wife. We were preparing to move back to Little Rock soon. There was no way she was going to live in town, having to face the neighbors after I fired one of them. She made me wait two months until we had moved! Personal issues got in the way of doing business the right way.

My senior management and executive experience occurred in high-technology companies. Most of my career, I worked in employment markets where skilled employees were hard to find. In addition, these were growing companies, and we needed to bring in effective new employees rapidly to support that growth. Throughout the 1970s, '80s and '90s, information technology employees remained scarce. Growth demand and shortage of people with IT knowledge led businesses to create attractive employment environments and creative new incentives to attract and retain these professionals. Rapid salary increases, bonuses, market-based pay ranges, frequent evaluations, career planning, training, education, tax-free savings plans, and rapid advancement became commonplace and expected.

During that time, many companies offered what became the "Mother of all Benefits": incentive stock options. Options were an opportunity to create significant wealth as companies prospered. A high level of compensation and attractive benefits became so commonplace that employees began to disassociate employment terms from business necessity. Many employees began to think of these unprecedented levels of compensation and benefits as an entitlement, which they were not. Finding appropriate employees and compensating them adequately is a business necessity; providing sufficient funding for a good lifestyle is not. Businesses pay what they must for labor required to perform their services. They should be expected to follow all laws, prevailing wage trends, and even common decency; but market supply and demand will always dictate the level of compensation and benefits.

Sluggish business conditions dominate today's employment market, resulting in tight expense controls and an oversupply of high-tech labor. Jobs are much more difficult to find and to hold. The United States faces a significant danger of losing many high-pay technology jobs to foreign markets. We can anticipate these conditions will stagnate compensation in disciplines where lower cost alternatives are available. I do not mean to downplay the unique value of high-technology employees, but the high levels and rapid growth of compensation for these employees in the last 20 years have resulted directly from business value, not individual skill.

A significant productivity difference exists between information-technology employees of high skill and those of average skill. While I have never seen this documented, I've observed that a highly skilled person will at least double the output and quality of the average employee. In Systematics, we focused a significant amount of the company's capabilities on employee selection, compensation, and development. We created these practices under the banner of another Walter Smiley phrase, "Fewer, better people." We achieved success with this approach, convinced our ability to create more value than our competition tied directly to workforce productivity and a relatively high number of these productive employees. Our employees at times lost this point, but we provided high levels of compensation to find the people that could generate high performance. This high level of performance proved so significant, we could afford a few mistakes. This reasoning had little to do with human relations. It was strictly business. This approach made us more competitive.

I have to assume this productivity advantage applies in any technology-centered business, although I only have direct experience in IT. Employers in these types of businesses have gone to great lengths to identify, recruit, maintain, and incent technology-oriented employees. Unfortunately, it is almost impossible to develop compensation that rewards only the highly productive. This search for the best has increased overall compensation at unprecedented rates, creating an employment market where people have come to expect high pay. I believe that in many cases, management misunderstood the compensation motivation that created this market. Without a productivity advantage, providing high compensation is bad strategy.

In the chapter *The Role of Money*, I discussed my first experience with large-scale layoffs as a responsible executive through implementing 1987's Black Monday at Systematics. For that time, the layoff was professionally and humanely done with an excellent severance package, simultaneous conversations with the employees being laid off as well as those remaining, a sound strategy for the future with clear objectives and measurements, as well as a client communication strategy. But it was also depressing, morbid, incredibly sad and the result of a complete management failure! The business result proved a positive shot in the arm for Systematics, brought significant profit improvement, refocused business leadership, improved client relations, revived career opportunities, and started another sustained growth period. But I still remember the feeling of failure.

We faced similar circumstances at Systematics on two occasions in the 1990s after the Alltel acquisition. I also participated in the same manner in layoffs at both companies where I served as an executive after I left Alltel. In all of these cases I fortunately was allowed to remain. The cuts were made for the benefit of the shareholders, remaining employees and even the customers, but we all felt like failures! (One conclusion might be to just avoid working where I do.)

Unfortunately, my experience is all too common in business, as the radical re-adjustment of cost structure happens with too much regularity over a business's life. Large layoffs are the result of a management failure. I can now see that infrequent radical readjustments result when businesses do not make constant adjustments. Keeping a tight control over expenses, monitoring employees' performance, addressing problems immediately, eliminating unprofitable business segments, re-evaluating business strategy and changing to adapt to market conditions are all necessary parts of business leadership. However, like most actions of human nature, they are rarely done in a perfect manner.

For me it was impossible to go through these layoffs without being affected by my actions' negative impact. Some people still hate me for firing them, and hate my former companies for letting them down. Yet I've also positively impacted other people's lives. Both my efforts, and more significantly the companies' efforts, have allowed workers to live a comfortable lifestyle, support families, and enjoy significant personal accomplishment. The feelings generated by these results, good and bad, are personal. But the work we do that generates them is not. It is just business.

Chapter Summary:

- Because operations and sales departments have different missions, measurements, compensation, behaviors, personalities and temperaments, they are frequently the source of internal conflicts. These are natural and normal conflicts, called "points of instability," that exist in all businesses.

- All employees are expendable. Of course some are more critical than others; but even the most important workers can be replaced, and the company will survive.

- It is important to realize this: workable strategies, sound business models, sufficient investment, competitive offerings, attractive markets, and dedicated leadership all go hand in hand with the hard work and good people required to build a successful business.

- A key factor for successful individual business performance is the ability to separate personal issues from business issues.

- You must distinguish between friends and business associates. Business acquaintances and co-workers are not friends. It is okay to be friendly with them; in fact, that's desirable. But do not make the mistake of assuming these individuals are friends.

- Businesses pay what they must for the labor required to perform their services. They should be expected to follow all laws, prevailing wage trends, and even common decency; but market supply and demand will always dictate the level of compensation and benefits.

- A significant productivity difference exists between information technology employees of high skill and those of average skill.

- Companies offer high levels of compensation to find the people that generate high performance. The value of this high level of performance was so significant, we could afford a few mistakes. This reasoning had little to do with human relations; it was strictly business.

- The radical re-adjustment of cost structure happens with too much regularity over a business's life. Large layoffs result from a management failure.

- Keeping a tight control over expenses, monitoring employees' performance, addressing problems immediately, eliminating unprofitable business segments, re-evaluating business strategy and changing to adapt to market conditions are all necessary parts of business leadership.

Teaming and Trust – The Basics

From my experience, the most significant transition from academia to business occurs with change from individual to group measurement and performance. School concentrates on each student's achievement, starting with the grading system's individual measurement. In addition, early in school we compete with our fellow students. Only a few students achieve top grades; almost all testing is individual; college admission is limited to certain students; only a specific number of scholarships are awarded, etc.

Most of us carry this individually centered belief system into our working lives. Our experience with groups, or teams, is usually limited to sports, clubs, hobbies, and special interest groups. These activities center on recreation rather than work.

Almost all work is a team exercise. Though many work-performance metrics are individual centered—such as salary, bonuses, incentives, performance goals, and evaluations—the ultimate measure of business success (return for investors) is absolutely a team accomplishment. The team includes sales, operations, customer relations, engineering, development and all the other functional areas that make up a business. If they function well together, the business earns profits; if not, difficulties always arise.

In business, you'll find no individual performers. Everyone depends on someone. Still, this very simple concept remains so difficult to learn. Most of us have become hard-wired for individual performance. Learning to work with others, trust others, support others and depend on them: therein lay a difficult series of lessons some people never learn.

Certainly one of Systematics' most remarkable characteristics during its glory years involved minimal investment in sales. For many years, the company spent less than 1% of its revenue on sales expense. For over a decade, there were virtually only two sales people, David and Hunter, both early hires as the company was forming. These guys were experienced ex-IBMers, strong-willed and knowledgeable about bank operations, data processing, sales, and contract negotiations. Both quite successful, they earned more money in good years than any other Systematics employees, including the CEO. Neither was pleasant to be around. No-nonsense, intense and focused, they seemed to operate independently from the rest of the company. You did not want to get in their way. If ever non-team players, yet successful people, existed in a company—behaving counter to my earlier emphatic statements— these were the guys! At least they seemed that way.

Sales people frequently develop individual-performer reputations. They are measured and paid based upon their production, with results appearing individually achieved. Their compensation structure, company role, and even personality type lead them to be task-focused, even self-focused and not too concerned with any issues but those affecting their sales. Still, I submit that even sales people are not individual performers, at least not good ones.

Many years later—after working closely with hundreds of salespeople as well as selling some on my own—I continue to respect, admire and even marvel at David's and Hunter's work. They created long-term deals that became the company's financial backbone. Pushing the company to escape its comfort zone of providing services in exactly the same way, they made us respond more uniquely to potential customers' needs. But they always took care not to push us too far, i.e. beyond our capabilities (although sometimes only with Herculean effort).

As the company operational representative, I would frequently travel with them to meet prospects. They'd present me as the person responsible for delivering the promised results. Both David and Hunter, particularly Hunter, would build me up as a brilliant bank computer operations expert, of highest character, always able to make things happen. I found that embarrassing, because I did not have all those capabilities. Here's what I did not realize: In that role, I was a sales *team* member. David and Hunter were expertly creating, coaching and leading groups of us as sales teams—an orchestrated effort to not only deliver a sale, but prepare to subsequently deliver the service. You can bet this successful sales effort involved team activity; and the team included people representing operations, development, client relations, training, human resources, technical support, executive leadership and administration.

Good sales people recognize their work's "team nature," even if the teams are small and only provide administrative support. Careful not to make enemies, they tend to implement an almost humbling, self-deprecating style. It encourages people to want to work with them and help. In the long run, completely self-focused, arrogant, solo sales practitioners almost always fail.

One of Systematics' many transitions included the introduction of several ex-IBM sales employees, most acquaintances of a new CEO. Trying to lead the company into growth, he segmented the organization into individual businesses to be measured by their profit contribution. A common organizational approach, he had seen it used at IBM. For a large number of financial institutions, Systematics provided account processing services based on a core set of application software developed in-house, under a constantly funded research and development budget. As a consequence, Systematics customers always expressed keen interest in how the company spent (if you think about it, THEIR) R&D money.

Focused on growth markets for services, we constantly reviewed needs for new software, and looked for banking-industry opportunities where we could apply technology to our customers' benefit. In the late 1980s, we increasingly concentrated on intelligent workstation software and equipment to communicate with core application systems. We wanted to improve and expand the capabilities of bank customer-contact employees. The most common contact points were the teller window and the new account desk, or "platform." As a result, new teller and platform systems were entering the market, and adding this capability seemed a logical expansion for Systematics.

Our CEO assigned responsibility for creating, marketing, selling and distributing this new capability to one of these newly recruited ex-IBMers. To protect the innocent, I will refer to him as Chuck.

An articulate, nice-looking, sales-oriented employee, Chuck clearly possessed high career aspirations. At that time, I was responsible for much of Systematics' existing customer relationships. These were long-term contracts generating the bulk of our revenue and profit. Chuck was to be measured on sales of this new platform and teller system. The quicker he could get something to market, the better, from his individual point of view. I remember an intense strategy meeting where we discussed this new product. Chuck was introducing to the rest of the company his plan to create and implement this product.

In order to get to market quickly, Chuck had chosen a partnership approach that would make the product expensive for much of our large client base. I challenged this approach, saying we needed to develop a system capability giving our clients some advantage and return on their existing investment with us. Efficiently and seamlessly mating this new capability with our existing software would significantly delay its speed to market. Chuck responded intensely to this challenge. He claimed these customers were not unique, and we needn't accommodate them because this was a separate product, and "I have to build a business!"

I still get mad when I think of those words: "I have to build a business!" He meant, "I must succeed with my assignment. I do not care about the rest of the company!" Chuck fell into a common business trap—the push for individual success at the expense of co-workers or the business as a whole. To give him credit (because he is not a bad person), I assume he believed if he performed as his measurements encouraged him to do, the whole company would benefit. That, unfortunately, assumes that executive management—who sets the organizational structure, measurements and incentives—can do so in a way that benefits the entire company. In many circumstances, that is not the case. Decision makers often inappropriately design an organization to compete with itself, to the company's detriment. For the most part, single business units measured by their profit frequently encourage this "individual" behavior.

In the 1990s, the individual business unit concept found increasing favor with organizational strategists. Under this approach, businesses were divided into smaller, manageably sized units intended to foster creativity, entrepreneurial behavior and team strength. In my experience, while a sound concept based on success stories, it is easily misapplied. The smaller business segments become fiefdoms, with leadership's primary goal to beat the other business segments. This creates an internal focus where measurements are all-important.

By definition, an internal business unit's measurement is an artificial creation based on assumptions. It can too easily direct energy and effort away from an appropriate external focus on customers. You must craft the organizational structure so that the individual pieces fit together to accomplish the company's overall mission. And this crafting must include tight standards and controls on individual flexibility. Otherwise, these structures inevitably fail.

What should you do if you find yourself in a company with measurements that create a competing organizational structure? You must work within the system, eventually reaching the point where you can influence or even change it.

To accomplish this, I believe the best rule is common sense, better described as common business sense. Always question what you are doing in light of its benefit to your customers and the company as a whole. When faced with a dilemma of your individual success versus the company's, choose the company. Then make sure you have thoroughly explained your choices and actions. In the long run, working for the company's common good is the right choice. Any sound leadership will appreciate a team player who passes up individual gain for company gain.

It is easy to understand the concept of playing for the company team's benefit over personal gain. However, it may be difficult to recognize the team. Who is on it? How should I prioritize my effort? Is part of the company more important? The best strategy: Consider the overall company influencers as top priority and yourself as bottom. Then fill in all the organizational structures between you and the top in hierarchal order. In other words, using current language, prioritize as follows:

Investor

Customer

Company

Division

Business Unit

Team

Self

What team are you on? All of these. But placing priority in this manner will most benefit the business, and therefore—in the long run—you.

Co-workers who are not team players are common, and always uncomfortable to deal with. Companies are teams. Individual performers do not fit, and will eventually cause failure. I believe this is an inherent part of the system, and non-team players eventually work themselves out of a job. This line stands out in Shakespeare's Merchant of Venice: "...but at the length truth will out." Which means ultimately truth will reveal itself and prevail. This is a fact in business. Poor team players' behavior—if understood by the company system (management, co-workers, subordinate employees, customers, suppliers, etc.)—will lead that same system to eventually boot them out. This only happens if the system is *aware* of the behavior. So the best way to deal with them involves making sure their actions are observed and not hidden. Then let the system take care of them. Essentially, this is a communication problem. Adequate communication leads to clear understanding, and clear understanding lets the system work.

The heart of successful teaming in business, and I guess the heart of all successful relationships, is trust. Trust is a by-product of consistency, predictability, common objectives, respect and, unfortunately, time. You *earn* trust by always doing what you say you will do, and by working for the common good, rather than just your individual welfare. You know from your own relationships: there are some people you trust, and some you do not. You also know how hard it is to regain broken trust. Your first goal in business: become someone who can always be trusted, and begin earning that position immediately.

Walter Smiley frequently preached short sermons on trust with a lecture about friends versus enemies. As Walter would say, "Everyone you deal with in business is either a friend or an enemy....either they are with you or against you. You need to decide which category each person you deal with fits, and deal with them accordingly." This clearly communicates the importance of trust, and of understanding who you can and cannot trust. I have trouble with the black-and-white concept of classifying people as enemies. I even think business circumstances sometimes affect behavior. On occasion, people may do things that make them seem like enemies; but their behavior is influenced by their business circumstances, measurements, contracts or directives. Still, the clarity and value of this message is sound. Trust is vital. Either you have it or you don't. Care about it! Earn it!

This discussion of teaming and trust leads us back to the issue of friendships in business. It is clearer to think of this in terms of business acquaintances and personal friends. While it is okay to have personal friendships in a work environment, they can make conducting business more difficult. To simplify this statement, we base personal friendships on caring and concern for people, deep feelings that lead us to look out for them and put their interests above ours. Business relationships exhibit a pleasant sort of social compatibility, but are based on respect, consistency and ethical behavior. You must make business decisions first for the business, and close personal friendships just get in the way. It is hard enough to demote, pass over, or fire a business acquaintance. To do that to a personal friend is gut wrenching, and likely the end of the friendship.

It's difficult to separate personal and business friendships because it is not *natural*. We naturally want feelings associated with all relationships to seem personal, and take precedence over business logic; that can create problems in the conduct of business. Certainly, your ability to make decisions for the good of the business first is a learned skill. Even when the relationships are close and personal, business demands that you meet its needs first. You must learn to prioritize your thinking and decision-making to support the needs of your company, its investors and its customers before accommodating the needs of your business acquaintances. This prioritizing of thought represents your growth in business maturity.

In addition, business relationships naturally vary in intensity in direct proportion to the amount of business contact. In other words, you may develop a great, close working relationship with team members. But expect that relationship to wane if you change to another team, and you are no longer in direct business contact. Do not take this change of relationship personally. It is neither good nor bad. It is just the nature of business.

Business is nothing more than managing and negotiating a series of relationships. Individuals contribute to a business, but they do so by contributing to the performance of a team; and teams are the heart of business. Trust, which you must build and earn, is the foundation for participation in relationships, and the basic element of successful teamwork.

Chapter Summary:

- In business, there are no individual performers. Everyone depends on someone.
- Good sales people recognize their work's "team nature," even if the teams are small and only provide administrative support. In the long run, completely self-focused, arrogant, solo sales practitioners almost always fail.
- Decision makers often inappropriately design an organization to compete with itself, to the company's detriment.
- The measurement of an internal business unit is by definition an artificial creation based on assumptions. It can too easily direct energy and effort away from an appropriate external focus on customers.

- You should always question what you are doing in light of its benefit to your customers and the company as a whole. When faced with a dilemma of your individual success versus the company's, choose the company.
- Poor team players' behavior—if understood by the company system (management, co-workers, subordinate employees, customers, suppliers, etc.)—will lead that same system to eventually boot them out.
- Adequate communication leads to clear understanding, and clear understanding lets the system work.
- Trust is a by-product of consistency, predictability, common objectives, respect and, unfortunately, time. You *earn* trust by always doing what you say you will do, and working for the common good, rather than just your individual welfare.
- Your first goal in business: become someone who can always be trusted.
- You must make business decisions first for the business, and close personal friendships just get in the way.
- Business is nothing more than managing and negotiating a series of relationships. Individuals contribute to a business, but they do so by contributing to team performance; and teams are the heart of business. Trust, which you must build and earn, is the foundation for participation in relationships, and the basic element of successful teamwork.

Communication – How Do You Do It?

My former employer Acxiom Corporation, a technology services provider, pays outstanding attention to its employees, *associates* in Acxiom's language. Fortune magazine selected Acxiom as one of the 100 best places to work for five years out of a seven-year period beginning in the late 1990s. Geographically disbursed, Acxiom spreads 5,000 associates over seven major locations, in addition to several smaller offices and a large number of home-based associates. A heavy user of today's new communication tools, the company implements email, voicemail, teleconferencing, videoconferencing, webinars, even psychological testing. Acxiom places a strong, and I believe admirable, emphasis on improving the working relationships between its associates, even dedicating a corporate function—organizational development—to improving associates' interrelations.

For a number of years, Acxiom was as good an employer as you could find; but, like all of my previous employers, communication problems ran rampant. Invariably, if an issue existed with a customer, internal department, team, project, leadership, or almost any part of normal company function, poor communication sat at the problem's heart.

In technology companies—or any company's technology-oriented department—employees' black-and-white, literal nature, along with their generally poor verbal skills, create problems. Much of hi-tech industry's service business today remains nothing more than an interpretive position between technology creators and users. The service consists of an understanding of the business problems and issues, subsequently redefining these problems and issues into a form that technologists can understand and use—i.e., clearly defined product requirements and specifications.

In a similar manner, companies that produce hardware and software usually succeed in direct proportion to their ability to communicate their offering's capabilities in the user's business terms. Frankly, lucrative career opportunities exist for people who can master the transition between the worlds of business and technology through their communication skills.

Even though our tools are different today, with email, conference telephone calls and PowerPoint heavily emphasized, poor communication still stands out as a major business problem. Tools are not solutions; they just allow the problem to morph to a different form. The best rule of thumb: Always communicate as if you were face to face with the person, or persons, involved. Written communication can seem impersonal, but it's permanent. Never write anything down that you would not be willing to say face to face.

When I refer to communication, I mean speaking, writing and listening. These basic human interpersonal skills create the basis of information flow and understanding, which make them a key factor in all business transactions. They also, of course, represent a key factor in all relationships, and are therefore just as important in our personal lives. Since communication is so personal (we all do it), I believe we tend to think we communicate well, and are frequently surprised when people do not understand us. People, though generally with good intentions, often possess a self-centered world view that others can never completely understand.

Invariably, when problems occur in business, you can trace them back to a communication issue where clarity and an open exchange of information would likely have prevented the problem from occurring. By far, the best way to communicate effectively involves putting yourself in the other person's position. Then base your communication on making sure they clearly understand, rather than on what you alone consider clear.

My sister, Marty Nord, works as a communication consultant, primarily with technology-oriented businesses. She trains executives, showing them how to successfully deliver messages through writing and speaking. She built her career springboard from almost 20 years of teaching writing and communication skills to engineering and business students at Vanderbilt University. Marty frequently dealt with technical students' communication stereotype, basing her negative example on "my brother, the engineer." Some of her stories were real, but examples of poorly communicating engineers are so common, all the tales were believable. Her goal was to keep engineers from acting like engineers. She and I are both convinced that even small communication-skills improvements pay big dividends for employees in every discipline.

Your approach to communication, in other words your communication style, stands as much a part of your personal definition as the way you look, dress, or your knowledge. I submit that in business, your communication skills represent the clarifying characteristic that defines you as a person. Communication lines up right behind character and integrity, which are not always visible. Communication style can even define what you do. This reality is so clear that business people frequently define other business disciplines by characteristics that reflect communication styles.

Communication style often combines with business personality types to create predictable behaviors that have evolved into stereotypes. While stereotypical behavior reflects the roles and responsibilities of functional positions, improved communication can break the stereotype. Have you met any of these yet? If not, you will:

1. Technical people (engineers and all forms of programmers) are too literal and see most issues as "black and white." They do not understand, or even care for subtlety, and therefore are not helpful for making sales, comprehending business value, negotiating, completing deals, or anything requiring compromise or business judgment. Always finding that more needs to be done, they never complete a project.

2. Top executives do not understand what is actually happening in their businesses. Their "reality" view of shop-floor activity, or what the products and systems really do, or what employees think, or what customers need seems superficial and uninformed. Of course, top executives usually learn from their own employees, so their view becomes distorted by what the company tells them. Usually, the more layers of management, the

more out of touch they are at the top.

3. Customers do not know what they want. They keep changing their minds, even when we give them exactly what they asked for.

4. Sales people just do what the customer says, even when it is unreasonable. They also do not understand our capabilities, or what is and is not acceptable risk. Sales people do not work hard, and they make too much money.

5. People in accounting do not understand what it takes to make a sale, cut a deal, complete a project, or even run a business. They are humorless and only can see the numbers.

6. Lawyers are deal killers, interested in pontificating and dwelling on unimportant issues.

The above behaviors, exaggerated and unfair, can all be identified as stereotypes containing strong elements of truth. Communication is the key to breaking down stereotypes. As I think of the best engineers, senior executives, sales people, accountants, and other professionals I have known in business, the best ones invariably possess outstanding communication skills. Good listeners, they take time to understand others' viewpoints, respect other people, and do not take themselves too seriously. As you move into a functional role in any business situation, take time to learn the stereotype, and then make a strong effort to minimize those behaviors. You will become a hero!

When I went to work for Systematics, I moved from manufacturing to data processing, a significant cultural/environmental change that exposed me to a unique and confusing language. The acronym-laden, non-verbal communication environment of data processing proved difficult to comprehend. It was literally months before I could understand what these people were talking about, and I still struggle today. While part of the problem remains technical people's literal nature, I became convinced that they spoke in code because they did not want others to understand them. For many years, non-technical people have perceived technology businesses as mysterious. This lack of understanding leads to job stability for those providing technological services.

Accepting this unique language has become a necessity to work with technical people, but it also pegs them as stereotypes, limiting their value in business. Even in technical companies, the leadership must understand and communicate in the languages of finance, law, human relations, marketing and sales, as well as technology. All these disciplines have formed their own languages. The only way to bridge the gap between them is to simplify the language to a common denominator. The best leaders I have known developed the ability to communicate to different disciplines, in language each could understand, and to simplify complex issues to salient points.

Make your goal that clear ability to communicate at all organizational levels. The best way to develop this skill involves avoiding unique language. Business lingo is unnecessary, immature, and symbolizes a lack of understanding.

Lingo appears to develop in cycles, and new words constantly arise to explain the same issues. Just for fun, a couple of years ago during three days of Acxiom meetings, I recorded a vocabulary that I considered silly business/technical terms. I've listed them below. This is not an indictment of Acxiom; most companies share this problem. With a little listening, you can probably create your own glossary of poor terms—language that will mark you as a follower. Do not use it!

EXHIBIT 1 - CURRENT BUSINESS SLANG

1. Think outside the box – Intended to define creative thinking, not restricted or constrained by standard norms or behaviors.

2. Connect the dots – Actually comes from the same "leadership" exercise as "outside the box." Implies following available clues to their logical conclusion.

3. Business pains – Issues in a business that cause problems. I envision a person doubled over in agony because sales are low!

4. Right People on the Bus – Refers to hiring the "correct" people for the company, and choosing acceptable people to join any particular project.

5. Do the math – Researching and understanding an issue to reach a logical conclusion. Can refer to numerically measured issues, so that understanding the measurements will lead to a logical conclusion. Can be a directive statement... "You do the math"...typically insulting. Or a reference to sufficient background work for a certain conclusion, "I did the math!"— which is bragging.

6. Pinged – Requested information from. Derived from the technical language for computers that send a signal to other computers or devices, searching for a return signal allowing the initiation of communication. Typically used by technical people, and characterizing the user as a technical person.

7. Enterprise – An entire business, inclusive of all of its functional parts. Another term I hate. For me, there is only one Enterprise, the starship.

8. Sales Engine – A group of people dedicated to performing sales work. Could consist of sales reps, sales managers, sales support, etc. Refers to a successful sales capability. Usually the context is positive. I've never heard a reference to a stalled sales engine, or a blown one.

9. Raise the Bar – Set performance goals at a higher level, or improve performance. Way overused, it should be relegated back to the high jump in track and field where it belongs.

10. Go to the next level – What you do after you successfully "raise the bar." It implies transcending through improvement to the next measurable set of objectives and capabilities.

11. Business Rules – The customer's unique specifications for a particular business need. Well-defined business rules could be crafted into programming specifications, thus creating systems to accomplish the tasks defined in the rules. Acxiom uses this term to classify work that we don't understand, and therefore it's the customer's problem.

12. Tailwind – Flying term implying when a given activity is succeeding. Synonyms include "momentum" and "picking up steam."

13. Traction – Ideas creating adhesive friction, and then gaining momentum. In other words, ideas begin to be accepted, or projects begin to succeed.

14. Drink the Kool-Aid – You agree, reluctantly. Ridiculous reference to the ritualistic suicides of James Jones' followers by drinking poisoned Kool-Aid.

15. Dashboard – Series of performance-measuring reports. Just as a car dashboard displays the gauges allowing you to monitor the engine's performance, this dashboard provides the information necessary to monitor a business or project.

16. Top of Mind – One of the more important issues to be dealt with, or an issue of major concern. Sounds like, and is overused by, consultant-types.

17. Long Pole in the Tent – Step in a project or process that takes the most time, particularly management time. Also, an item whose timing is critical for successfully completing an activity. This phrase conjures up all kinds of silly images. When I hear it, I immediately forget the subject and start thinking about the circus.

18. White Space – The unknown or incomplete parts of a plan. Comes from the blank space left in a spreadsheet or matrix used as a planning document.

My first experience with business-communication training involved a behavioral-science course in undergraduate school. Our grade was partly determined by writing and presenting a paper. The presentation would be videotaped, with a subsequent review and critique. I was terrified. I had done little public speaking, most of it poorly. I had never seen myself talk except in front of a mirror, and I was not too pleased with that. I bet I gave that presentation to myself twenty times. The students were required to watch each other perform. That just increased my fear. I made it through the presentation okay. But, to my surprise, the professor's review was actually good. Not great, mind you, but I looked much better than I "felt" during the presentation. That little exercise gave me some confidence. I still remember it today when I have to present a talk. Of course, it went well because I was prepared, and had practiced many times.

Communication skills are learned behaviors, and can improve through training. Without practice, they deteriorate. Staying current requires focused work. In our church, services begin with a congregation member leading a responsive reading of the liturgy, part of the Call to Worship. Each week a different person leads—a simple way for members to participate. This may only take two or three minutes, with just a small number of lines read solely by the leader.

Tom Bonner, a local public-relations executive and long-time television weatherman, is a member of our church. One Sunday morning before services began, I saw Tom standing in a corner of a classroom, practicing reading aloud. When I got closer, I realized he was reading from the bulletin and, sure enough, he was the liturgist that morning. This guy is a former TV personality. He makes his living speaking, and does this in some form every day. And he was practicing before reading a small part in church! If he needs to practice for something like this, I need a major overhaul before I stand in front of anyone. The lesson: We all need to work hard at being better. Never stand up in front of a group and talk if you have not prepared well.

The presentation tools we use today, particularly PowerPoint, have made it easy to develop attractive visual aids that can improve the quality of presentations. Unfortunately, these images have become so easy to create, presenters frequently overuse them; so the images have become a distraction from delivering a clear message. If you have not already, you will likely have the opportunity to sit through someone's 50+ slide PowerPoint pitch. The slides are nothing more than lists of words used as the speaker's notes, and the speaker reads them. These presentations may greatly induce sleep, but fail to deliver an effective message. Even worse is the complex, multi-colored, flow-chart slide. The speaker proudly proclaims that it clarifies the workings of a complex system. The lesson: In a presentation, only use flowcharts that are easy to read. Build them sequentially through the talk.

Effective slides reinforce the speaker's point, capture the observer's interest, and tell a story. Use them sparingly, and only to support an overall message.

The key: Thoroughly plan the presentation specifically for its audience. What are you trying to say? Why are you saying it? What difference will it make to this audience? What do we want them to leave with? What are the measurements of a successful presentation? What do you want to happen?

You must know the answers to these questions before you ever stand up and talk in front of any group. In business, or any meaningful group communication in life, this is serious. Any group. Any time. Successful presentations accomplish their intended purpose.

Preparation makes successful presentations. It shows respect for the group, and for yourself.

I have reasonably succeeded over the years in bridging the communication gap between the functional areas of businesses where I have worked, as well as between users and developers. I do not pretend to know it all. Libraries of information and training are available on this subject. But here are some of Collins' Communications Rules. Follow these and you will become better—not perfect—but better!

1. Think about each communication before doing it, and plan the best method to accomplish your purpose. What am I trying to accomplish? How will this be perceived? What is the best way to have this communication? All communication should be for a purpose, and all communication has a secondary impact beyond its initial execution. The observer will perceive it one way initially, but likely in a different manner after reviewing it again from notes, or even just thinking about it later. You want to make sure this secondary impact does not negate the purpose, or worse, come back to haunt you.

2. Always handle sensitive, "sticky" issues one-on-one in private. Do not fight battles in public. That behavior destroys trust in you. Never target negative comments to people, either directly or by innuendo, in open forums (common areas, meetings, etc.).

3. Never send an email if personal conversation is a reasonable option. Never send a string of emails back and forth to the same person. Stop after two and have a conversation.

4. Email is not private. Even worse, it is legally discoverable. Never argue or be emotional in emails. Never use email for communication you are not willing for others, beyond the address list, to see. Always compose emails with the assumption that someone other than the addressees will see them.

5. Never send more copies of emails than necessary. Confine this communication to people with a need to know. At times, "need to know" is a broad group and email is an effective tool; but a good general rule is to limit the distribution.

6. When giving negative feedback, to help ensure people hear it, give positive statements first. For example, "I like the way you do 'X', but....." In fact, in working with humans of any age, the same techniques apply.

7. When you do not agree with someone, focus on the behavior and not the person. This is critical in business, as the objectives and driving forces are rarely personal. We just think they are. Try to understand the motivation behind behavior. Often people are doing what they believe to be right, and clarifying the circumstances and viewpoints becomes a way to approach a middle ground.

Use a communication hierarchy as you work with people in business. Knowing that clear and effective communication is always the goal, use the best possible communication that fits the circumstance and time available. Always put extra effort into trying to be clear in any of these mediums.

I rank effective communication methods as follows, with the best at the top:

1. One-on-one in person, private conversation –the most personal method of communication, and the one least likely to result in misunderstanding. The participants gain the benefit of voice, inflection, facial expression, body language, and privacy to clarify their message.

2. Personal telephone call – In my experience, the introduction of email has lessened reliance on the telephone call as a primary communication method. This is unfortunate. The personal call can be quite effective because of the nuances delivered through voice, tone and inflection.

3. Text Message or Instant Message – As you will notice from this list, I believe communication that is personal and focused between individuals is generally more effective. Text and IM are exchanged in real time, are quick (assuming you can type), and are more personal than email because they are targeted between individuals. However, like email they are legally discoverable. You should therefore exercise care that you do not record information you do not want others to see.

4. Email – It has revolutionized business communication, and is an excellent way to deliver a consistent message clearly and quickly to a large number of people. It should force the writer to think carefully before creating it. Generally, when taking more time with a message, you can be more precise. The problem: it is impersonal, and unless superbly written, can be difficult to interpret consistently. As stated earlier, it is also discoverable for legal reasons, and may therefore be read by many other people than originally intended.

5. Voicemail – Obviously only a one-way communication, but does allow the advantage of voice with time independence.

6. Hand-written note – Not suitable for quick communications, but a very effective way to deliver a personal and targeted message.

7. Hard-copy memo – Since it has to be physically handled, hard copy is slow in all forms. However, a memo is perceived as more casual than a formal business letter. It can therefore be effectively used for a permanent record of a more personal message.

8. Hard-copy letter – In today's business world, hard copy, formal business letters are somewhat infrequent. They're primarily used for official business communication where record-keeping and legal interpretations are important. Most hard-copy letters verify communication that already took place using another medium.

Your communication skills will determine your success in business. Your cleverness and intellect won't overcome an inability to communicate. In fact, the opposite is true; a superior ability to communicate can help overcome a lack of intellect! The good news: You can improve communication skills. Thoughtful preparation, including selecting the appropriate communication method, will make you a better employee, and a leader.

Chapter Summary:

- If an issue exists with a customer, internal department, team, project, leadership, or almost any part of normal company function, communication sits at the problem's heart.
- Lucrative career opportunities become available for people who can master the transition between the worlds of business and technology. Communication skills are the basic tools required.
- Never write anything down that you would not be willing to say face to face.
- When I refer to communication, I mean speaking, writing and listening. These human interpersonal skills form the basis of information flow and understanding, which make them a key factor in all business transactions.
- Invariably, when problems occur in business, they trace back to a communication issue where clarity and an open exchange of information would likely prevent the problem.
- In business, your communication stands as the clarifying characteristic that defines you as a person.
- Communication is the key to breaking down stereotypes. As I think of the best engineers, senior executives, sales people, accountants, and other professionals I have known in business, the best ones invariably developed outstanding communication skills.
- Accepting technology's unique language has become a necessity to work with technical people, but it also pegs them as stereotypes, limiting their value in business.
- The best leaders I have known could communicate to different disciplines, in language each could understand, as well as simplify complex issues to salient points. Business lingo is unnecessary, immature, and symbolizes a lack of understanding.
- Never stand up in front of a group and talk if you have not prepared well. Successful presentations accomplish their intended purpose. Preparation makes successful presentations.
- Think about each communication before doing it, and plan the best method to accomplish your purpose.

- Always handle sensitive, "sticky" issues one-on-one in private.
- Never send an email if personal conversation is a reasonable option.
- Never argue or be emotional in emails. Always compose emails assuming that someone other than the addressees will see them.
- Confine email distribution to people with a need to know.
- When giving negative feedback, give positive statements first.
- When you do not agree with someone, focus on the behavior and not the person.
- Your communication skills will determine your success in business. You can improve communication skills. Thoughtful preparation, including selecting the appropriate communication method, will make you a better employee, and a leader.

Humanity in Business — Humane Behavior

I love this topic…Humanity in Business. What is that? Is there any? What difference does it make? Does anyone care? I submit that strong humanity exists in business, but only because business is made up of humans. At times, business will appear inhuman, cold, unfriendly, and even cruel. It can also be funny, captivating, challenging, motivating and thoroughly rewarding. In short, for most people, business represents a major life experience—the source of much of their structure and most of their economic livelihood. But business is an artificial structure, with rules based on finance, not humanity.

The human side of business reveals itself through individual behaviors, not defined by the business game's rules. In other words, businesses exist for a financial purpose, not a human one. But human behavior's dynamics define predictable business rules. In effect, business experience involves learning how to understand and predict these behaviors, as well as learning the art of influencing them for the business's ultimate gain.

By "humanity" I mean human behavior, with a synonymous implication of humane behavior. This discussion will explore how people behave, with some "dime store psychology" references to why. Throughout this discussion, always keep in mind that business's driving forces and purpose are financial. They have nothing to do with treating people well, or allowing them to achieve their personal objectives. Those may be good strategies that pay off profitably, but they are not the purpose of business.

For most of us who work in a business, our role involves helping the business accomplish its financial objectives in exchange for our own financial rewards in the form of compensation. However, employers and employees' complex relationship involves more than just a financial exchange. As a result, a business's internal work is largely dedicated to optimizing human interaction. In the more formal sense, this optimization becomes the role of management, with the available support of staff functions, particularly Human Resources. Of course, everyone who works in a business should consider it his or her job to optimize human interaction. In the long run, that makes for a more enjoyable life and is good business.

I see the world's "glass" of life as half full. I lean toward optimism, looking for the positive in most situations. I'm not suggesting everyone should hold that viewpoint, but it's probably an easier path to choose, even in difficult circumstances. I also believe business people generally want to do a good job, and try to do the right thing. But their viewpoint, background, knowledge, perspective, leadership and even resources vastly differ, resulting in wide performance variations. Know that business people do what they do for specific reasons. Understanding those reasons will improve your ability to work with others, significantly helping your contribution to the business.

With Systematics, I eventually held positions where I could work with our customers' senior executives. Prior to that time, I feared executives, a view shaped by my earlier roles. I perceived them as holding power over me, an assumption likely rooted in my own insecurity. For the most part, I've had positive experiences with executive leadership, particularly CEOs, in large organizations. I've found them easy to talk to, focused on business, and reasonable about conflict issues. Invariably, their business sensibility and ease with communication didn't carry over to their reputations, but it has been my experience. To clarify, when dealing with business executives, I've been either an employee or a customer/supplier. Particularly in those latter cases, I always tried to prepare well when meeting executives, respecting their time. With that caveat, I find people in these positions easy to work with.

I can't always say the same about middle management and, in many circumstances, the CEO's immediate leadership circle. I've found a common organizational phenomenon surrounding a CEO: the creation of an insulating structure; i.e., people who do the CEO's dirty work. Some of the more difficult, arrogant and self-focused business people I have met play this middle management, filtering role. Their actions define a CEO's reputation, and getting around them can be a political chore.

When people are unreasonable in a business environment, they usually have a business reason. For the most part, people don't want to be jerks, but in some cases their organizational role strongly influences their behavior. As a supplier, our path to CEOs often became restricted by people whose organizational role was to "block suppliers from top management." By the time we made it through to the CEO, we had passed a number of gates of acceptance, and were consequently welcome.

At Systematics, we included in-house legal counsel as standing members of our negotiating teams. The complex nature of our long-term outsourcing relationships required thorough documentation of each party's responsibilities and liabilities. As a result, our lawyers became not only skilled specialists, protecting us in our contractual relationships, but also excellent sales people and mediators. They were fully engaged, competent, professional members of our business-development teams.

Our first in-house lawyer, Jim Wilkins, proved outstanding in this work, an amazing wordsmith who was thoroughly respected by customers and opposing legal counsel. I continue to have the highest respect for Jim's professional ability. He has gone on to gain national prominence and recognition in an outsourcing-contract law practice.

A number of months after Alltel acquired Systematics, the Alltel in-house legal team began examining the Systematics in-house lawyers' work. Systematics routinely made certain contractual commitments to its customers that Alltel questioned. In addition, we were asking for more legal assistance to support an increased workload. In the course of this review, I became involved, along with Jim Wilkins, in renegotiating one of our large customer's agreements. In reviewing this contract, Alltel lawyers subjected Jim to some of the most degrading, dehumanizing verbal affronts I have ever witnessed in business. They insulted and berated him in a manner I found hard to believe.

At the time, I couldn't see why they were attacking Jim. He was quite calm through this experience, but I thought their behavior was unacceptable, and it made me angry. Now, after 15 more years of experience, I see this situation from two perspectives.

On the one hand, and from a purely business viewpoint, this represented an example of one internal department exercising its power over another. Alltel's lawyers likely wanted to gain control over a strong and influential part of Systematics' leadership, possibly by creating an environment that encouraged Jim to leave. If so, they succeeded. Jim eventually moved on to a specialized practice bringing many achievements and recognition. In my view this was a loss for Systematics.

The Alltel lawyers involved in this review are usually good people, also adept at negotiating contracts with customers. They are quite "humane" in other business and personal settings. In this case, I believe their assignment involved gaining control over Systematics' legal staff, a valid business objective for an acquiring company. I do not agree with their approach, and believe they could have met their objective in a more humane and direct way. But no matter what I think now or thought then, in the end they obtained their desired result. So from their point of view, this represents another behavioral example of the maxim, "It ain't personal, it is just business."

Sometimes business objectives are hard to obtain in a humane way. Some personal suffering is inevitable. This does not mean the people involved are bad or inhumane. Obviously some people are better at dealing with difficult subjects in a humane way than others. I believe that, if you're skilled and open about the reality of business issues, you can minimize the inhumane side of business execution.

However, the other lesson in this story, beyond business sometimes being difficult and impersonal, is that you do not have to be a jerk to do it. This same business result could have been obtained with open, direct, frank and honest communication about the actual issues involved. Your jerk behavior tends to come back to haunt you later in your career. It also introduces a stress on co-workers and on the perpetrator's mental health that is damaging and absolutely unnecessary. Don't be a jerk.

Unfortunately, you'll run into some jerks in your career. For purposes of this discussion, let's call a person exhibiting abusive, condescending, arrogant, demeaning, or some form of self-focused and self-important behavior a jerk. You may have another list of adjectives that apply, but you know what I mean because you know how you "feel" when you work around them. If you're forced to deal with someone who exhibits jerk-like behavior, that's no reason to immediately quit or refuse to work with that person. You should never participate in an emotional exchange with a jerk. On the contrary, remain calm, professional and factual in your interactions. An ability to temporarily disassociate yourself from your feelings gives you an advantage. Some people call this acting.

The jerk's role in your business relationship is important. If he or she is someone you serve, e.g. a customer or investor, you should work to elevate your "jerk tolerance" to a higher level. In Systematics, the intense, time-dependent nature and broad scope of our in-house department's responsibilities made us a frequent criticism target. In a few circumstances, our middle management contacts would act like jerks to us as they received co-worker pressure about some aspect of information technology. Such positions, where you become a focal point for communication over which you have minimal control, can prove frustrating, and likely lead some people to jerk tendencies. One of my best Systematics leaders described this situation as the "Everyone needs a dog to kick syndrome." Sometimes our role as an in-house supplier required us to accept blame for problems, taking heat off certain individuals in the customer organization. In other words, we could accept a little abuse since we were being paid well to provide the service—a business-to-business example of "the customer is always right."

If the jerk is a co-worker, minimizing contact may be the best alternative, but it's not always possible. I believe the best way to deal with a jerk co-worker is through one-on-one private, personal conversation to discuss the specific behavior that disturbs you. Possibly the person doesn't realize your negative reaction, will truly be sorry, and your relationship will improve. Your honest criticism in private will show you understand what is happening, will not tolerate it, and possess the rational, practical ability to do something about it. This will also likely help your relationship improve. You must discuss specific behavior and how it affects you, not just snap, "You're a jerk!"

Of course, the problem multiplies if the jerk is your boss. If you are fortunate enough to be in a rapidly growing or progressive company, invariably you will change bosses frequently. Then the best solution may be to tolerate the jerk a while because you'll soon move to a new boss. That one-on-one private conversation I discussed earlier can work with a boss also. I actually experienced this once with great success. The boss habitually berated individuals in group meetings. When he blasted me, I considered it an ineffective way to persuade me to do anything. I confidentially told him so. That did improve our relationship, and I think positively affected his behavior in other circumstances. That conversation took place later in my career when I was less concerned about consequences, but it proved the right thing to do.

If your company has an open-door policy, as many do today, you should take advantage of it. Speak to a higher level manager about your intolerable boss. Many employees are afraid to take this step, afraid of retribution by their boss. As in the earlier one-on-one conversation, carry on a factual and unemotional discussion, describing the circumstances precisely. You have a right to be heard, and the manager will seriously consider your petition if you avoid personal accusations. All the companies where I worked that had open-door policies were serious about them, wanting them to be effective. Never tolerate a boss's retribution after an open-door conference. If your company claims to have this open-door communication and appeal process, but then allows retribution, you should strongly consider working elsewhere.

Only you can decide acceptable behavior in your dealings with others. Only you can set your personal level of tolerance. You may judge a situation intolerable for personal reasons. My advice: Do not approach these situations lightly. Make every effort to act in the best interests of your company and your customers first. If you decide leaving is your only option, start looking for alternatives confidentially. Do not tell your co-workers. If at all possible, only leave after you have secured another position. When you tell your company you are leaving, speak factually and honestly about your reasons. But do not openly accuse the jerk of being one. Just frankly and unemotionally describe the situation you find intolerable. State that this creates a working environment you find unacceptable, and conclude by saying you will be moving ahead. Make it simple, straightforward, honest and clear. That is the high road.

This is what Jim Wilkins did in the situation I described above. He acted with dignity and class, leaving only when he found an excellent alternative and that the company could manage without him. We can all learn from his example.

The most prevalent inhumane behavior in business today involves job loss. It does not matter whether it is a firing, layoff, reduction in force, job elimination, merger, forced retirement or any other synonym. Unplanned job loss is serious and painful to everyone involved. Anyone who participates in it should understand that it's inhumane. I contend that forced job losses represent management failure, but I also accept that, at times, the losses must occur.

I worked with a Systematics manager, brought in from IBM by our CEO, who was smart, articulate, a creative thinker, a good manager, and a knowledgeable technology executive. He was also noticeably ambitious, blunt, and direct. Peers and co-workers often perceived his interpersonal style as condescending. He created frequent conflicts and alienated many of Systematics' managers. His style also led people to challenge him frequently, as well as question his value to the company. Although I did not agree with his approach, for the period of time he worked for me, I learned to appreciate his intellect, sincerity, and overall contribution to the company.

At one point, we had to cut costs, leading to significant layoffs. His negative reputation and questioned value made him a prime target for job elimination. I kept him employed through a round of layoffs by some vigorous arguing about his capabilities. Of course, he never knew this.

In less than two years, more cost cuts required layoffs. This time my arguments didn't succeed, and his name went on the cut list. Recognizing my strong advocacy, our CEO offered to substitute for me in the layoff conversation. However, I believed that since the manager worked for me, it was my responsibility.

The conversation went poorly. He had many strong negative comments about the company, its leadership, our future, and me. I lost a business friend in this process, which I strongly regret. But I also believe I did the right thing, even the most humane thing, both by defending him and then letting him go. I played within the rules, doing all I could to help the business. In the final analysis, these are every business person's responsibilities.

We want to work with people who are confident in themselves and their business positions. This confidence stems not only from their personal mental health, but also their clarity regarding their organizational role and its value. When people are unclear of their role or value, or if they are fighting to prove their worth (e.g. saving or justifying their job), they can become non-communicative and even combative. This is particularly dangerous in a career's early stages. As you strive for advancement, you can become easily focused on some end objective. You may not recognize or appreciate the value of a slow journey, made in the right way. It is easy to quickly dismiss, or even run over, any issue or person that gets in your way.

I have found the best strategy: Treat *everyone* with the highest respect. I really mean *everyone*....co-workers, superiors, employees, customers, suppliers, literally everyone with whom you interact. People have a way of resurfacing in key roles later in your career. They define you by your communication, primarily displayed in your interaction with others.

Do not fall into the trap of taking yourself too seriously, pushing others aside for your personal gain. That approach will not work. Instead, do everything you can to make your company, and your co-workers at every level, successful. You will be rewarded innumerable times both monetarily and psychologically. In simple terms, be one of the good guys!

Chapter Summary:

- The driving forces and purpose of business are financial, and have nothing to do with treating people well, or allowing them to achieve their personal objectives. Those may be good strategies that pay off profitably, but they are not the purpose of business.
- Everyone who works in a business should consider it his or her job to optimize human interaction. In the long run, that makes for a more enjoyable life and is good business.
- People do what they do for specific reasons, and understanding those reasons will improve your ability to work with others and significantly improve your business contribution.
- People who are unreasonable in a business environment usually have a business reason. For the most part, people don't want to be jerks, but in some cases their organizational role can strongly influence their behavior.
- Sometimes business objectives are hard to obtain in a humane way. We have to accomplish them for the good of the business, but some personal suffering is inevitable.
- If you're skilled and open about the reality of business issues, you can minimize the inhumane side of business execution.
- Jerk behavior tends to come back to haunt you later in your career. It also introduces a stress on co-workers and on the perpetrator's mental health that is damaging and absolutely unnecessary.
- If you're forced to deal with someone who exhibits jerk-like behavior, that's no reason to immediately quit or refuse to work with that person. You should never participate in an emotional exchange with a jerk. On the contrary, remain calm, professional and factual in your interactions.
- I believe the best way to deal with a jerk co-worker is through one-on-one private, personal conversation to discuss the specific behavior that disturbs you.
- Only you can decide acceptable behavior in your dealings with others. Only you can set your personal level of tolerance.

- We want to work with people who are confident in themselves and their positions in business. This implies not only their personal mental health, but also clarity of their organizational role and its value.
- The best strategy: Treat *everyone* with the highest respect. People have a way of resurfacing in key roles later in your career.
- Do not fall into the trap of taking yourself too seriously and pushing others aside for your personal gain. Instead, do everything you can to make your company, and your co-workers at every level, successful.
- Be one of the good guys!

Humanity in Business – Personal Motivation

What is your motivation in business? What is anyone's? Is everyone the same? Are individual motivations mutually exclusive? Can you get yours only if someone else doesn't get his or hers?

I see two significant driving forces that push individuals in business today: compensation and the desire for a meaningful career. Let's face it, many of us "professionals" like to talk about the motivation of personal fulfillment, contribution to society, recognition, winning and many other soft rewards; but a job's compensation stands as the necessary prelim to all other forms of motivation. Our business needs may parallel Maslow's Hierarchy of Needs (Table 1), with basic survival aligned with employment, and self-actualization the ultimate result of career refinement. In other words, if you don't have a job, all the soft stuff doesn't matter. We use compensation to satisfy our need for security. Until we take care of that, we don't have time to worry about the rest.

TABLE 1 – MASLOW'S HIERARCHY OF NEEDS

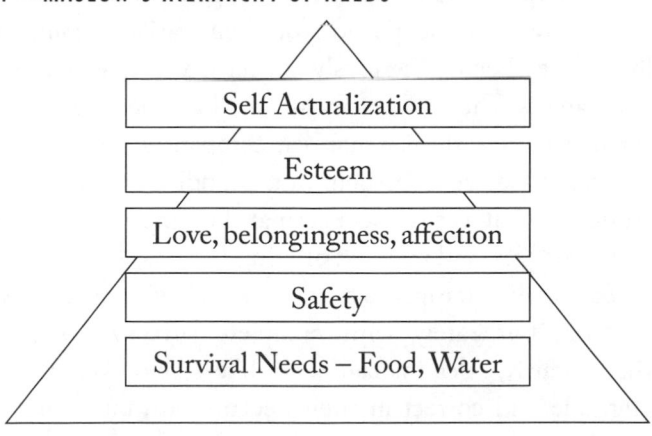

Self Actualization

Esteem

Love, belongingness, affection

Safety

Survival Needs – Food, Water

We became professionals as a strategy to satisfy basic needs. As a result, we all anticipate we can find work. With the basic security need covered, we can focus on "adequate" compensation and fulfilling our career aspirations. Most of us fall in this category. We're concerned about compensation and intend to make sure it is adequate over time. In addition, we strive for work that satisfies us, meets personal objectives, and in the long term improves our self worth and contribution to society. But we should remember business's hierarchy of needs, and that threats to lower levels of need make the higher levels unimportant. If you do not believe me, ask anyone who just lost his or her job!

Business compensation incentives represent a thoroughly flogged topic with lots of available expert opinion. Companies invariably micro-manage incentive compensation to control employee behavior. For the most part, these efforts don't work as anticipated. Frequent changes in incentive compensation methodology create a sure sign of management ineptitude. This phenomenon is particularly common in sales compensation.

Management typically constructs sales compensation with a higher variable, or risk, component and lower fixed compensation. Sales people are comfortable with this compensation structure, and willing to risk lower guaranteed compensation for the opportunity to earn more money. Companies willingly go along with this structure because they only pay large amounts when the appropriate revenue is available to cover the compensation expense. Most sales people count on receiving some portion of their variable compensation annually; so they become seriously concerned if they believe they'll miss their targets. They always focus on what's necessary to receive their payments. In a similar manner, companies use this need for compensation to drive sales behavior, prodding the sales force to concentrate on whatever is of concern at the time, such as prospects, customers, products, and targeted offerings.

I've seen many attempts to refine sales behavior by manipulating compensation, but rarely with complete success. To generalize somewhat unfairly, sales managers are like economists; they sound knowledgeable and correct in their declarations, but rarely are. As opposed to economists, and unfortunately for the sales discipline, it's easy to measure sales-management quality through revenue achievement or the lack thereof. It can often result in high turnover of sales managers!

The reason is simple. Sales people concentrate on their compensation plans every day, constantly seeking angles and loopholes to positively impact their measurement. Sales managers consider these plans once or twice a year. They can't possibly keep up with the interpretations their employees will develop. I don't claim to be good at setting these incentives, but I am convinced that sales people outsmart their bosses most of the time, primarily by paying attention.

As a result, if you see a company changing its sales plans annually, management likely doesn't know what it's trying to accomplish. No doubt, simple measures are easier to understand, more predictable, and in the long run more effective. For sales people, by far the best measure is revenue. In addition, targets should be difficult, but not impossible, to obtain. The art of sales management involves setting the target, not crafting the plan.

For operational employees, "operating profit" represents the best incentive target. Operating profit is controllable by the individual manager being measured. It therefore includes revenue for the products/services delivered, the team employees' salaries, their additional expenses, any equipment or software necessary to deliver the work, and little else. These operational measurements should not include allocations for non-controllable expenses (e.g. corporate overhead) or charges from other internal departments (e.g. IT), unless these charges are controllable.

Many companies manipulate their incentive plans through internal measurements to "net profit." "I want to see the true contribution of this work group," is the mantra you will hear to justify this arithmetic exercise. The problem with this thinking: It focuses the manager being measured on allocation method, leading to inordinate concern about internal issues. I've seen hundreds of hours wasted in endless meetings and political manipulations regarding the method of calculating internal profit for measurement purposes. This kind of internal concentration saps energy and destroys focus, detracting from the important mission of helping customers, generating revenue, and controlling costs. Don't be fooled by the logic. These thoroughly defined internal profit measures do not work!

However, talking out of my mouth's other side for a while, aligning company and employee interests through financial measurements and compensation is an important management tool that companies should strive to achieve. It's also difficult to accomplish over a long period of time, and therefore rare.

What's the most effective alignment of company and employee financial objectives I have seen? Stock options. When this works right, employees focus intently on the shareholders' measurement, and true employee wealth-building can occur when the company meets its shareholder objectives. In growing companies, these options—spread over a large number of employees—can minimize negativity and create an energizing focus on results. Still, stock options are not a panacea. They can become irrelevant to employees in a serious down market.

What's the most successful "non-equity" way to accomplish this alignment? In my experience, it's tying some significant portion of incentive compensation to the company's financial targets on an annual basis. The important factors are consistency of plan across the employee base, consistency over time (e.g. do not change it every year), and results achieved. In other words, if employees don't gain some measurable benefit, the value is negative. But if these plans are executed well, management can achieve the ideal of all employees pulling for the same objective.

For a broad plan that includes all employees, I believe the measure should be profit. Frequently, lower-level employees have an excellent sense of how to save money, and for sure understand when it is wasted. Most organizations do a poor job of tapping into this excellent knowledge source. However, when all employees' compensation is tied to company performance, more employees will willingly speak up with opinions about how to improve it. If the company isn't able or willing to listen to its employees, this form of compensation can become counterproductive.

I worked with an acquired company that offered an incentive bonus plan for all employees based on revenue and number of employees. This incentive was paid every year, and all employees expected it as a portion of their compensation. So getting hired by this company was difficult. The existing staff worked hard, even taking on extra work voluntarily to prevent additional hiring, because they saw every new employee as money out of their pockets. This company was admirably efficient, and obviously paid attention to its employees.

Incentive pay that isn't paid becomes a disincentive. In recent years, many companies have lowered salary expense in response to generally poor economic conditions. Along with layoffs, management frequently uses restructured incentive pay plans to moderate compensation expense. By lowering fixed compensation and raising the variable compensation of incentive pay, employers can decrease salary expense until improved business conditions make higher compensation affordable. Most of us relate to poor business performance in slack times. We're temporarily willing to sacrifice for the company, usually as long as the job market is tight, or about two years, whichever is longer. I don't claim this outcome to be precisely measured; but plans such as these become counter-incentives if they don't soon result in actual pay.

Where compensation fills Maslow's lower needs, our "career" parallels the higher needs. You wouldn't be reading this book if you didn't want your work to satisfy more than the basic needs of survival and safety. It's likely you expect your chosen career path to also help satisfy your need to belong, to feel good about yourself, contribute to a higher cause, and become the best that you possibly can. These higher levels of need satisfaction are your responsibility, not your employer's. While the purpose of business involves generating a return with a financial measurement, your purpose in working is broader than financials, and frankly, more important.

You work to survive first, but also to fulfill your life and contribute to society; to make the world a better place, and support the fulfillment of your highest calling. For most of us, the higher calling will be dominated by relationships, those of family and friends, as well as spiritual. This higher calling is also characterized by a balance between your work and personal life. A sound work life supports and enables you to pursue personal and family dreams, philanthropy, and even the time and resources to focus on relationships.

A successful career is not life's ultimate goal, and those who treat it as such are ultimately disappointed. Because of the time and energy the early stages of a career demand, your first few years of work are a dangerous personal time that requires a conscious effort to keep your life in balance. Do not fall victim to the easy path of career first, everything else second. There are both direct and subtle encouragements in business to work until you drop. It is all too common to hear management speak reverently of employees who defy odds and accomplish significant results through their intense efforts. There is an implied pressure to take on any work available, and volunteer to do all that is necessary to accomplish a desired result. In a similar vein, business people will brag, either directly or in a pseudo-complaining style, about how hard they work, the implication being, "I am better than you because I work harder!" Do not fall victim to this siren.

To be blunt, leaders who perpetuate this all-work myth are unreasonable and unwise, and business is full of them. I was one for a number of years. I now see many friends and co-workers that seriously damaged their physical and mental health, as well as that of people close to them, by this selfish, business-only approach to life.

Listen to me here. All through your career, make a conscious, planned effort to balance your work and personal life. In the early stages, put additional effort into making sure you have a personal life. Be aware that early in your career you will have to work very hard. You are learning. You will make mistakes and have to correct them. You will be thrilled at making money and want to make more so you can buy "stuff". You will feel the weight of family and personal responsibility.

These are all important messages, but you are responsible for putting work in the proper perspective, and balancing it with the rest of your humanity. This does not mean you only work 8 to 5 and never on the weekend, because the focus of work demands will require more time than that. But there is no honor in the 80-hour week. It will kill you.

Like much of business, this balance is an art. Know the potential danger of an all-work life. Plan to avoid it through balancing significant relationships, active participation in your family, a healthy lifestyle, and voluntary contribution to society. This, my friend, will save you.

Chapter Summary:

- A job with compensation is a necessary prelim to all other forms of motivation. If you do not have a job, all the soft stuff is unimportant. We use the compensation of work to meet our need for security, and until that is taken care of, we do not have time to worry about the rest.

- We strive for work that is satisfying, meets personal objectives, and in the long term improves our self worth and contribution to society. But we should remember business's hierarchy of needs, and when lower levels of need are threatened, the higher levels are not important.

- If you see a company that changes its sales plans annually, its management likely doesn't know what it's trying to accomplish.

- For sales people, by far the best measure is revenue. The art of sales management is in setting the target, not crafting the plan.

- For operational employees, "operating profit" works best as the incentive target.

- Operational measurements should not include allocations for non-controllable expenses (e.g. corporate overhead) or include charges from other internal departments (e.g. IT), unless these charges are controllable. This kind of internal concentration wastes energy and destroys focus, detracting from the important mission of helping customers, generating revenue and controlling costs.

- Aligning company and employee interests through financial measurements and compensation is an important management tool that companies should strive to achieve.

- The most effective alignment of company and employee financial objectives is through stock options. In growing companies these options, spread over a large number of employees, can minimize negativity and create an energizing focus on results.
- The most successful "non-equity" way to accomplish this alignment is to tie some significant portion of incentive compensation to the company's financial targets on an annual basis.
- Incentive pay that isn't paid is disincentive.
- You work to survive first, but also to fulfill your life and contribute to society, to make the world a better place, and support the fulfillment of your highest calling. This higher calling is also characterized by a balance between your work and personal life.
- A successful career is not life's ultimate goal, and those who treat it as such are ultimately disappointed.
- Leaders who perpetuate this all-work myth are unreasonable and unwise, and business is full of them.
- All through your career, make a conscious, planned effort to balance your work and personal life.
- Know the potential danger of an all-work life. Plan to avoid it through the balance of significant relationships, active participation in your family, a healthy lifestyle, and voluntary contribution to society. This, my friend, will save you.

Improving Your Value

In the chapter *How Do I Get Started*, I declared that early in your career you are not hired for your knowledge, but rather your ability to learn. School plays a role in establishing your career by making you more valuable, but maybe not in the way you thought. It's not so much what you learned in school that makes you employable; but rather school allows you to prove you possess a certain intelligence level, certain skills and, most importantly, an ability to learn. Companies hire you for what you will do for them in the future. They are willing to invest in your future learning with them because they believe you will add value to their business.

In this situation, both your employer and you have a common interest: Your ability to add value makes you more desirable to your employer as well as others. In fact, I'll make the case that, if you cannot add value to your employer's company, you do not belong there. If your personal goal is to increase your level of responsibility and compensation rapidly, and build wealth over time, your goal for your company should be to increase your level of contribution. In other words, perform work that makes your company more valuable, make money for them, and you should expect rewards.

As I discussed briefly in the chapter *The Role of Customers*, when I started with Systematics, we were just completing development of a commercial loan system as an addition to our suite of banking software products. Immediately after my orientation, I spent a few months in our software development division, ostensibly helping out but actually trying to learn, as well as stay out of the way. I was assigned to the commercial loan team, which was frantically trying to finish this complex system so it could be installed at a customer site. This was my first exposure at Systematics to the intense amount of work required to support an aggressive sales organization struggling to generate growth in a dynamic and demanding competitive environment. We had committed to good customers that this system would possess certain functions and be finished on a specific date. No matter what happened, we had to honor those commitments, even if some people had to work until they dropped!

In those days, the system component invariably receiving the least attention and quality effort was its documentation. No one wanted to work on documentation, and we had almost no clue what good documentation contained. Therefore, given the axiom that crap travels downhill, and with my role as a new management-trainee starting at the bottom, documentation became my assignment. I actually worked on the end-user documentation, writing explanations of all the system's input forms, output reports, and their use. A weak candidate for this role, I had never worked in a bank, and didn't have a clue how the system would be used. But I could write well for an engineer, and was willing to ask questions, which made me a relatively good choice.

Actually, once I got started, I found the subject of commercial lending interesting, so I approached the task with lots of energy. To write the documentation, I had to learn every field in the system, along with every line item on every report, and how it was produced and used. When I did not understand something I would ask about it, particularly trying to comprehend what was important and why. Literally, this work made it possible for me to become an expert on this system's content and use in a relatively short time.

My knowledge of how to implement the system quickly brought me into customer exposure as our commercial loan system was being converted in a second location. I joined the implementation team in a training/communications role with the client. This system conversion was successful because of the development team's Herculean effort. I was fortunate to be associated with that hard-working group. That conversion, and the information I learned, led me to more opportunities for training users and presenting the system's capabilities to customers and potential customers.

While this exposure and work opportunity may seem like no big deal, it was important for me. I did become an expert through some extra effort on my part, and the fact that the system I learned was commercial loans became my good fortune. As it turns out, commercial lending is the primary profit engine for commercial banking, typically led by the bank's most powerful executives. My knowledge of this system enabled me to gain exposure to important senior leadership in our customer organizations, and I was able to help them through their use of this system. That knowledge, along with our commercial loan system's positive contribution, benefitted me throughout my Systematics career. I could talk intelligently with bank CEOs about their business. This helped me gain some distinction as a technologist who understood their business and could add value to their organizations.

It's important you know the lesson I learned by accident: Significant value exists in thoroughly developing your expertise in some area for your company. You should become an expert in something. It's wise to select an area either closely aligned with what your company does to make money, or one that represents particular value to your customers. In any case, that development of expertise will allow you higher-level exposure, and the subsequent opportunity to make contributions that others cannot. This will prove good for your company, and subsequently good for you.

Becoming an expert will set you apart from others in a positive way, and will likely result in higher-level job opportunities. Although it's not necessarily logical, when you demonstrate significant expertise in one area, you will invariably receive credit for having expertise in other areas. For example, "He has a good relationship with the commercial-loan executive; surely he would be a good choice to manage an overall banking relationship..." The truth may be that you do not have a clue beyond one particular area; you just "look" like you do.

At some time in your career, you'll be challenged to perform work you've never done before. You probably won't believe you can do it. If you are to advance significantly in your career, you must take advantage of these chances when they come. You must be willing to take the personal risk of moving out of your comfort zone. Expertise in some area will provide the ticket to these opportunities, and I believe it can be your ticket to success when it comes.

In my case with Systematics, I used my knowledge of our commercial loan system and a subsequent interest in banking, particularly lending, to deepen my understanding of our customers' interests and needs. I became a much better executive because I understood our services from our customers' view, particularly our customers' executives. That knowledge provided an advantage in every position I held at Systematics. It allowed me to remain credible even in posts where the primary task was technical, or financial, or behavioral. I knew what the customer wanted and why, and I could translate that into Systematics language.

As I've mentioned briefly, your choice of company roles can significantly affect your value, and subsequently your compensation and overall opportunity. Some roles are more important than others. In my experience, the highest value comes from roles engaging you in the unique work through which your company makes money. Make an effort to identify and understand your company's most important, most unique, and most valuable products and services. The quickest way to the top often is a path through these key offerings, one identifying you with making money for the company. Current popular business jargon would label this unique, moneymaking key a *core value proposition*.

In Systematics, that key involved managing on-site data centers that supplied banks with their mission-critical computer operational services. In Alcoa, the key was efficient manufacturing of their core product, aluminum, in its most profitable forms. I have worked around businesses where the core value proposition was customer relations, engineering, sales, marketing, and even financial management. This profitability key is not always readily apparent, and it may never be mentioned in their literature. You can determine it more easily from the inside as you begin to learn what's important, what demands the most attention and resources, what causes the strongest reaction when problems occur, and where the existing leaders came from. I'm not saying that this path through the company's most important sections is the only way to succeed, but it is the most reliable.

I have worked around a number of CEOs and other senior managers hired from the outside. Invariably, while smart people with successful backgrounds, many of them became notable failures for the same reason: They acted like they knew what to do when they did not. No matter how smart and successful you are, when you move into a new company, you must devote a certain amount of time and effort to understanding some basics: how the organization works, who's important and effective, who you can trust, what are the issues and obstacles to success, and particularly what are the business's unique subtleties.

My experience leads me to believe that senior managers hired from outside easily make the same mistake: They assume the company hired them for what they know, and to be in charge and accomplish something; so they better get on with it. The few leaders I've seen do this successfully spent an inordinate amount of time learning the company, listening to employees and customers, and building relationships with their management teams before taking any action. There is little room in a complex business for individual performers, and no room for them in leadership.

This same circumstance can apply to you. When you're assigned work that you are not yet qualified to do—and you will get that opportunity—you must *not* act like you know something you do not. It is acceptable, in fact I think it is desirable and endearing, to admit what you do not know and ask for help. Your best source of knowledge will be your co-workers and likely the people working for you. Ask questions. And when you do not understand, ask more questions. Be willing to listen, listen, and listen. In case you have not yet figured it out, the best way to listen is to stop talking!

When you advance in your career, requiring you to perform unfamiliar work you've never tried before, you'll find it advantageous to rely on what you *do* know. In other words, fall back. Rely on your strengths, the strengths that got you the opportunity in the first place. In my case, I had garnered knowledge of our customers' business, what was important to them, and how our company's actions affected them. Your strength may be in some other area, such as financial analysis, engineering, sales, marketing, strategy, or a combination of other disciplines. My point: You must work to learn how to combine your capabilities with those of your team. That is your responsibility as a leader. Frequently the key to success involves learning from others while relying on your strengths.

Never take yourself too seriously. Everyone you come in contact with has something to teach you. Give them that respect. Your co-workers will know what you can and cannot do before you will. Admitting your shortcomings, showing others respect for their knowledge and abilities, and working hard to help them overcome their problems—these actions will get your team on your side, and go a long way to ensuring your developing success.

Chapter Summary:

- Companies hire you for what you will do for them in the future. They are willing to invest in your future learning with them because they believe your involvement will add value to their business.
- Significant value exists in thoroughly developing your expertise in some area for your company. You should become an expert in something.
- When you demonstrate significant expertise in one area, you will invariably receive credit for having expertise in other areas.
- Some roles are more important than others. In my experience, the highest value comes from roles engaging you in the unique work through which your company makes money.
- No matter how smart and successful you are, when you move into a new company, you must devote a certain amount of time and effort to understanding how the organization works.
- When you're assigned work that you are not yet qualified to do—and you will get that opportunity—you must *not* act like you know something you do not.
- You must work to learn how to combine your capabilities with those of your team. That is your responsibility as a leader.

- Admitting your shortcomings, showing others respect for their knowledge and abilities, and working hard to help them overcome their problems—these actions will get your team on your side, and go a long way to ensuring your developing success.

Unwritten Rules – The Negatives

Much of what you learn in business comes through trial and error; you do something and see what happens. While I don't claim to be an expert, or long on wisdom, I have worked in business long enough to see patterns and cycles. I also have observed good and bad behavior, and frustrating repetition of the same learning process that wastes so much company time and energy. Invariably most people learn as I have. I want to believe it's possible to avoid common pitfalls and embrace successful behavior by learning from others' mistakes and successes.

Conventional business-speak includes much discussion of mentors—people with more knowledge and experience who work with younger businesspersons to accelerate their learning, and avoid costly mistakes. Some companies even formalize these relationships to develop workforce competence more rapidly.

I believe the mentor approach works well, recognizing we can learn much by listening to those who have worked and made mistakes before us. People in business tend to think their situations are unique. They use excuses such as market conditions, the economy, their industry, intellectual capital, size, differentiation from competition, or a thousand others. Some can fall into this trap, thinking their situation's unique characteristics make past experience irrelevant. I believe the art of learning through experience allows us to separate the unique from the repeatable, knowing when to listen as well as what to ignore. Committing to a belief in the similarity of business experience represents the correct approach. We can learn about solving today's problems by understanding what has worked, or been repeated, in the past.

With that nice introduction, I am compelled to share a short core dump of opinions. These statements about business will be obvious to some, but came to me only through years of trial and error. I wish someone had told me this stuff. Or more likely, I wish I had *listened* when someone told me this stuff.

1. *It ain't personal, it's just business* — I know this has come up in previous chapters, but I just cannot say it enough. If you take any one item from this book, this is it. While business's relationships and interpersonal behavior appear to mirror the rest of society, they are not based on the same rules or values. Investment drives business, and the measure of success is financial. Communication skills and relationships are critically important as means to accomplish a business purpose, not to make you feel good, become fulfilled, achieve power or make the world a better place. All of that may happen, but as a business by-product, not a purpose.

2. *There is no such thing as job security* — When I went to work for Air Products and Chemicals in 1970, I was assigned to a small welding-equipment subsidiary. Little did I know that group was not a successful part of Air Products. Soon after I got there, quite a few employees were laid off. I was terrified. Here I had moved my family all the way to Pennsylvania to start a "lucrative" management career, and people were losing their jobs. Obviously I had no seniority, and figured I would join the exodus. As it turns out, Air Products was not about to toss a newly hired college-grad, but I did not know that.

In my career's early stages, I wanted jobs with opportunity and power. Eventually, I became confident enough in my capability to not worry too much about losing my job. Young, aspiring professionals considered some jobs "safe": those with no likelihood of relocation or rapid advancement, but reasonably secure for a nice lifestyle with minimal pressure. Banking stood as the industry most often accredited with these characteristics. Some of my friends chose this path just for employment stability and security. Beginning in the late 1980s, economic and industry conditions turned that world upside down. Many bank employees lost their jobs to bank consolidations, turning this safe industry into one of the most volatile.

Deregulation has brought a similar impact. I know people in both the transportation and utility industries who have been forced from their once-secure jobs, left to struggle for alternatives in a declining employment market. Add to these experiences U.S. industry's drive for efficiency throughout the 1990s. It resulted in higher "productivity" (less people to do the same work) but destroyed any remaining sense of loyalty between companies and their employees. The bottom line: today's business conditions, industries, technology, and markets all change so rapidly, no one working in this environment can expect employers to take care of us. That is our responsibility.

3. *There is no such thing as being your own boss* — This one drives me crazy. It's such a frequent mantra among young professionals, and I was also infected with the "be your own boss" disease. Frequently, this claim is rooted in some problem with your boss, and a belief that you know how to handle some situation better. It is also fueled by realizing the large number of bad bosses out there, and the odds that you'll get some of them.

On the other hand, almost every viable business experience will situate you where you'll have to please someone—investors, customers, key employees, advisors, or any myriad others. Wherever you work, whomever you work for also has a boss. Your CEO will certainly answer to a board and investors. If you're inspired with a great business idea and receive funding from some source, believe me, you will be working for that funding source. If you work only on your own (not good job security, by the way) you will answer to your customers. In other words, you have to learn to get along, to understand what people want and need in a business context, to serve others and respond to them if you expect to succeed in business. You will always have to please someone. There is always a boss.

4. *You will never be completely prepared* — For much of my career, I have worked with technical people who performed tasks to accomplish some business result. Most commonly, this

scenario is characterized by creating and/or implementing a product or service, usually led in some form by a project plan. Good technical people are meticulous and thorough. Good project definition and direction includes all the steps necessary to ensure a positive result. Project planning's extent and sophistication has improved significantly over the last 30 years, but that sophistication has not necessarily resulted in improved performance. Technical people still tend to refine their work past the point of diminishing returns. Unfortunately, the realities of business make it almost impossible to completely create a new idea for market or implement a product/service for a customer— at least not as thoroughly as the project plan and the technical leadership will desire. In other words, the "build it and they will come" approach to creating products or services is not viable.

In practical terms, some art is always employed in the balance between initial concept, system design, customer expectation, market acceptance and willingness to pay versus project definition. In my experience, the sales discipline and the creation of a business-oriented result drive the process of developing new offerings. Rarely do we create new products or services with the creators' preferred finality. The end user should always come first.

5. *Businesses cannot save their way to prosperity* — In my work experience, I can think of at least six significant examples when my companies lost control over spending, resulting in severe cost-control measures including layoffs. In all of these cases, the problem resulted from a decline in profits, less than what we expected over two to three quarters. Also in all cases, business prosperity had caused us to take our eye off the cost-control ball. We allowed unnecessary expenses, particularly hiring. Actually, revenue flattened, and expenses continued to grow unchecked.

In these cases, we did what we had to do: preserve profitability by reining in expenses through layoffs, and raising the control level over all spending decisions. This necessary action worked well, and is a regular part of business's ongoing cycle. However, in each of these circumstances, a bigger problem than cost control existed—one related to revenue. Reasons varied, but the results were identical; we did not know how to increase sales and recover the declining growth rate. Our most serious problems involved lack of sales, sales-force quality, market awareness, product viability, and overall market conditions.

All companies should pay attention to cost control at all times, but that's just the entry fee to manage a successful company. Business prosperity comes from growth, and must be led by growth in revenue. Consistently investing in means and tools to grow revenue represents the heart of sustaining growth and increasing profitability. Implementing cost control can slow down or stop the bleeding, but will never cure the patient. You cannot save your way to prosperity!

6. *Business relationships are not friendships* — The heart of this issue relates to business's purpose and origin, which is financial, not personal. This is not to say you can't have friendships with people you work with, but it's critical to understand that business relationships are not friendships. These relationships may seem like friendships, e.g. they involve significant amounts of time, exposure, communications, and even trust. However, in the normal course of business, financial and competitive circumstances can create an intense and unfriendly environment. When that happens, friendships get in the way of good business decisions.

This problem most often surfaces when businesses are under pressure, particularly cost pressure. The most difficult manifestation comes when you need to reduce salary expense, requiring you to cut the pay of, or even lay off, a friend. But I have also seen friendships get in the way of promotion decisions, sales situations, business alliances and contract negotiations. The best way to approach this situation: First, understand that your friendly business associates are not personal friends. You should maintain good, positive, communicative, trusting relationships with your business associates, but avoid making them personal. In contrast, you should also recognize that any business activity with a close personal friend is treading on dangerous ground, possibly putting both your business and your friendship at risk.

In short, keep your business and personal life separate, with distinct boundaries. Do not assume you are different and you can manage it. The forces at work are natural and normal, and bigger than all of us.

7. *Business is not fair* — I have heard this comment frequently, particularly regarding business decisions made in reaction to some crisis. We can all probably accept that "life is not fair," but we typically say that cynically due to some series of events not working out well for an individual. In truth, fair is not a business term. Business's unfair nature isn't cynical; it's just the result of business's inherent set of rules based on its financial origin. We make decisions first for the good of the business, with financial measurement as the goal.

Still, while fair is not a primary driver, you should strictly adhere to "right" business behavior and avoid "wrong;" but prioritize that right and wrong behavior in a business context. Most all decisions regarding customers and employees, while they may end up being compassionate and fair, are done first for a financial reason and the good of the company. Since business practice is so dominated by relationships that seem personal (and it is important to be fair in personal relationships), you just inherently want business to be fair, and can become upset when it is not. That's not to say business is bad, because it's not. It's the economic engine that underpins the world's society, and can be meaningful, thrilling, fulfilling, and rewarding. It can also be cold, demanding, impersonal, cruel and devastating. Good businesses focus on ensuring sound financial performance, commensurate with growth. They will likely do that by responding to their customers' needs and treating their employees well. Fair isn't part of the equation.

Unwritten Rules – Growth

Growth is a problem. Now that's a dramatic statement about business, maybe even business-immoral. Actually, growth is an essential element of capitalism because it supplies the return investors require to participate. Without it, there would be no business. Eliminating my use of dramatic license, here's a better statement: Problems can arise with growth, and managing it is very difficult.

In my opinion, today's business environment worships growth. I say that in a negative context. I believe we strive to achieve unreasonable growth accomplishments, hoping for some kind of ultimate reward. Business measurements weigh the value of growth heavily, to the point that some people practice bad business frequently under the guise of facilitating growth. This is frustrating for us as individuals, because the system demands more growth each year, and that's inconsistent with human nature. The end result: This constant pressure for growth can only occur through a continual supply of more energy and creativity. For almost all of us, looking at this in a macro sense, our productive years will only result in a minor contribution to the business life cycle. In other words, feeding the business growth engine will eventually chew us up and spit us out. That's a built-in given of the process.

In my experience, the most common growth-related problems result from overly aggressive pursuit of revenue. This typically manifests in the sales organization's behavior, often committing to accomplish the impossible. Sales compensation is purposefully designed to stimulate adding new business, usually under short-time horizons. Hence the classic sales supervision lament: "But what have you done for me lately?" I believe the more serious long-term business problem associated with aggressive sales concerns the typical disconnect between sales and delivery. In other words, the immediate performance pressure on sales people encourages them to sell products and services the company is not prepared to deliver.

In like manner, operational people often don't understand the need to continually grow revenue. This leads them to resist the sales necessity of adapting offerings to the market's willingness to spend. This internal sales/operations relationship is a classic "point of instability" in business where there is never only one right answer. Managing this conflict is one of the many artful necessities of good business leadership.

I also believe that growth necessity leads to a condition where the successfully growing business operates just slightly "out of control". I do not mean this in a negative sense. In managing the point of instability between sales and operations, the force of sales is the best approach for creating a slight tilt toward the more demanding aspect of growth. Where do you think the term *sales force* came from!?! Seriously, the conservative nature of good operational leadership makes it difficult to rely on these leaders as a growth engine. I believe that responsibility will always rest with sales.

Growth also hides problems. In every layoff situation I've endured, a major part of our problem has involved costs rising faster than revenue. In all of these cases, the problem followed a period of excellent growth, where we were scrambling to keep up with sales. We let our control over spending get lax. As a result, when sales declined, our unchecked rate of spending continued. In short order, our profitability was wiped out. It is amazing how often we have to relearn that lesson.

In business you should spend money as if it were your own. Be careful not to commit to permanent increases in the spending rate without assurances that the supportive revenue is secure. In other words, be careful about hiring too many people and making large investments in physical plant and equipment. Always try to make do with less than you think you need, while you constantly monitor sales.

Too often our struggle to grow has led to inordinate risk, misaligning sales with delivery capabilities, eliminating long-term investment, and creative accounting. The late Paul Williams, one of

Acxiom's most quotable leaders, included the following mantra in every one of his presentations and discussions about our company's financial performance: "This is the most important quarter, ever, in the history of the Acxiom Corporation!" It became both a running joke and an expression of appreciation for Paul, but unfortunately it is true. Today's businesses, at least publicly traded companies, focus their management almost exclusively on quarterly performance. I believe we have carried this emphasis to the negative extreme. As a result, the long term planning and investment necessary to sustain healthy companies over time become difficult to accomplish.

My experience with publicly traded companies identifies an intense focus on managing quarterly numbers and an equally intense pressure to produce the "right" financial impact based upon expectations. I never saw any illegal activity. Quite the contrary in my experience, we applied as much attention to ensuring that our accounting practices would withstand audit scrutiny. On the other hand, I also observed a complete willingness to sacrifice the long-term for the short-term when quarterly performance was affected. This was never the strategic intent; but the market-demanded necessity to produce the expected quarter-to-quarter performance took an inordinate amount of management's time. It required an aggressive emphasis on closing sales with a similar amount of heavy-handed control on expenses. The fear of not posting quarter-to-quarter improvement represents a significant disincentive to investment. I believe it's the primary reason we see so few long-term successful businesses.

Here's another phrase attributed to Walter Smiley at Systematics: "The short term always takes precedence over the long term." That's a great example of business behavior. Invariably, when you confront any problem or issue, the most immediate solution will prevail. This is why people in an organization with strategic responsibility cannot also be held accountable for tactical results. For example, developers cannot be held accountable for day-to-day fixes. If they are, the result will be no development. This is human nature and a natural point of conflict.

The only resolution: Executive management should separate responsibilities between strategic and tactical work, and absolutely commit to honor that separation. The market's short-term pressure can become a dominating influence to these same executives. As a result, effective long-term leadership is rare.

The best overall company management results I've observed took place in private companies and limited-ownership public companies. These companies sustained positive growth in revenue and profitability over a long period of time. I attribute this condition to their setting a longer-term strategy and direction, and sticking by it even through negative cyclical results. It's unfair to be this simplistic because those positive returns resulted from many other factors; but I'm convinced I saw more unhealthy behavior in companies that managed only to the market's quarterly expectations.

Over the last 10 years, this has become a serious problem. I assume the 1990s' rising market—and the resultant broad participation of institutional investors, private investors and corporate officers—has intensified the seriousness of stock-price changes. The artificial boom of the 1990s' latter half— with the telecom and dot.com investment hysteria in particular—created false expectations about the potential of stock ownership. The inevitable return to reality then became a crash.

Just as stupid as most investors during those years, I did nothing to protect my equity holdings from the anticipated fall, instead opting for them to go "just a little higher." We all should have known better. I do not believe companies can sustain the growth necessary to support PE ratios over 25-30, and in fact do extremely well if they maintain ratios of 10-15 over time. Watch out for companies that depend on these high multiples, obviously as investments, but also as employers. You can bet cost controls are coming. You might as well be a professional gambler.

Much of today's business difficulty rises from the unsuccessful effort to manage growth; but that does not mean growth is unmanageable and unattainable. Some people will argue that capitalism and its inherent reliance upon growth are evil, but I don't reside in that camp. Just because it's hard doesn't make it wrong. I saw enough long-term, well-managed, consistent growth to remain both a business and capitalism zealot. I believe the issue comes down to following proven business practices.

My best experience with delivering consistent, profitable growth came when we engaged in sound fundamentals during an expanding market. In those cases, growth came from satisfying customers; understanding their needs; delivering cost-effective products; investing in improving our offerings over time; hiring intelligent, hard-working people; paying them competitively; developing their skills, and financially managing our business on close to a cash basis. This positive combination of circumstances was rare, but I did see it; and it was ultimately rewarding.

You and your career will be well served by always working to achieve these same sound fundamental behaviors, and insisting on them in your employer.

Chapter Summary:

- Growth is an essential element of capitalism because it supplies the return investors require to participate.
- Business measurements weigh the value of growth heavily, to the point that some people frequently practice bad business under the guise of facilitating growth.
- Feeding business's growth engine will eventually chew us up and spit us out. That is a built-in given of the process.
- The immediate performance pressure on sales people encourages them to sell products and services the company is not prepared to deliver.
- Operational people often don't understand the need to continually grow revenue. This leads them to resist the sales necessity of adapting offerings to the market's willingness to spend.
- The conservative nature of good operational leadership makes it difficult to rely on these leaders as a growth engine. I believe that responsibility will always rest with sales.
- In every layoff situation I've endured, a major part of our problem was costs rising faster than revenue. In all of these cases, the problem followed a period of excellent growth, where we were scrambling to keep up with sales. We let our controls over spending get lax.

- Too often our struggle to grow has led to inordinate risk, misaligning sales with delivery capabilities, eliminating long-term investment, and creative accounting.
- The fear of not posting quarter-to-quarter improvement is a significant disincentive to investment. I believe it's the primary reason we see so few long-term successful businesses.
- The short term always takes precedence over the long term. The only resolution: Executive management should separate responsibilities between strategic and tactical work, and absolutely commit to honor that separation.
- I do not believe companies can sustain the growth necessary to support PE ratios over 25-30, and in fact do extremely well if they maintain ratios of 10-15 over time.
- My best experience with delivering consistent, profitable growth came from situations where we practiced sound fundamentals in an expanding market.

Unwritten Rules – Wealth Building

Not only does growth drive the inherent reward for investors, it is also the engine behind personal wealth building, close to all employees' hearts. Company growth can stimulate broader responsibility, the key determinant for individual salary progression. In addition, compensation bonuses are typically tied to short-term growth. When I started working, eventually earning enough money to survive on my own, I slowly began to realize my compensation—even at the lofty levels I eventually hoped to achieve—would not build wealth. In this definition, *building wealth* is accumulating significant capital and assets to live a comfortable lifestyle, educate children, prepare for retirement, and protect from catastrophic issues such as illness or long-term unemployment. Without frugal, astute financial management, which is difficult to practice, salary will not suffice for wealth building.

Ignoring the best way to obtain wealth today (inheriting it), you build wealth through ownership. Ownership allows personal wealth to approximately track company value, which you expect to grow at a faster rate than compensation. If not, investors likely become dissatisfied, pressuring for change. Rank and file employees can find ownership elusive; but young professionals should aim for it, and make it a major consideration in career planning.

For this discussion, let's ignore the obvious theoretical possibility of starting your own business. Let's focus instead on what most of us do: work for someone. Lack of ownership potential is one of the major negatives of small, and particularly family-owned, businesses. While at times their rhetoric may imply otherwise, small businesses will not open ownership to you except under unusual circumstances, meaning you have something they must obtain. For your long-term career and wealth building, it's best to think of these businesses as opportunities to obtain broad experience. You can learn there, preparing yourself for positions in other companies where ownership is a better possibility.

The most common opportunity for company ownership comes from stock distribution to employees in publicly traded companies. This can occur through subsidized employee-purchase plans, grants, or stock options. I have seen few grants in my working lifetime, but have enjoyed benefit from both purchase plans and options.

Here's the ownership lesson I learned, actually by accident and good fortune: There's no such thing as getting rich quick through company stock-ownership plans. In the case of the small stock amounts companies can afford to offer employees, perseverance with a growth company is the path to reward. In other words, if you choose a company willing to share its ownership—an important behavior in the long run—your opportunities will come in small increments over time. The company's growth, when combined with frequent additions to your company holdings, can build significant wealth over a number of years. Expect to build wealth over 15-20 years, not just a few years. In this respect, wealth building can allow you to educate your children, upgrade your housing, and significantly subsidize your retirement—reasonable goals and expectations. What's unreasonable? Hoping to score a home run and quickly join the rich and famous.

Obvious keys exist to obtaining your reasonable goals. Select a company that's likely to sustain growth over time and is willing to share ownership with employees. In addition, you must be able to remain employed. To solidify your chances, I would look for financial strength, growth history, market presence and competitive position in your employer. Many companies encourage employee ownership participation through subsidized stock-purchase plans. These plans may seem like no big deal. But, if the company grows at all, the discount can become one of the best investment deals you will find. Sustained participation over a long time period remains the key to realizing this type of plan's benefit.

As of this writing, recent changes in accounting regulations and financial reporting requirements have negatively affected companies' ability to offer stock options to a broad employee base. Previously, employers could extend stock options to employees without having to recognize the option's expense until it was exercised. Firms had found it advantageous to grant a number of options as employee retention tools and no recognized expense. They'd only absorb a compensation expense if the employee stayed long enough to exercise the option, typically over five to seven years.

This regulation change does not damage broad employee-based company ownership's value to employers. It just changes the means available to obtain that value. I expect employers will meet this change by creating other manageable-over-time vehicles allowing employees to participate in company ownership. These may include discounted purchase plans, restricted grants, tax deferred accounts, retirement plans, or any number of yet-invented alternatives.

In this discussion of wealth-building possibilities, I'd be unfair to disregard small, privately owned businesses completely. You build wealth by the appreciation of owned assets. This seems simple enough. But, while ownership of stock in publicly traded companies is commonly available to employees, it's rare to gain ownership in companies not publicly traded. This kind of ownership will not be as liquid. Therefore, it can be difficult to ever turn into cash. Again, it's not impossible to find small, privately owned companies willing to share their ownership; but you should expect the search to be difficult. Business owners' willingness to let you earn a piece of their company over time represents your best indicator of their viability as long-term employers.

Ownership of small, non-growth businesses also can be a source of wealth building. But it's also associated with more personal risk than employment with a large company. Two of my friends pooled some of their assets, borrowed a considerable amount of money, and bought two well-established, family-owned printing businesses. These were certainly not growth businesses in the traditional sense. But my friends constructed a deal allowing the cash generated by the businesses to retire the debt over time. In this manner, they increased their ownership of the business asset, just as you would your house through a mortgage. For them, this effort eventually created a substantial asset, but not without significant personal risk.

These guys are experienced, financially astute business people—managers with enough personal assets to secure lending for their acquisition. The businesses they bought are demanding and competitive, and do not run by themselves. Their effort and risk is significant; but they are building their personal wealth in the true capitalistic fashion, and their effort and results are noteworthy.

It's important that you seek long-term employment with organizations that value your participation in ownership, whether they are public or private. Upon making that match, your focus should then move towards achieving the value contribution, along with the patience required to stick with that alternative over an extended time period.

Chapter Summary:
- Growth is also the engine behind personal wealth building.
- Your salary will not suffice for wealth building.
- You build wealth through ownership.
- The most common opportunity for company ownership comes from stock distribution to employees in publicly traded companies.
- You do not get rich quick through company stock ownership plans. Perseverance with a growth company is the path to reward.
- You should build wealth over 15-20 years, not just a few years.
- Small-business owners' willingness to let you earn a piece of their company over time represents your best indicator of their viability as long-term employers.
- Ownership of small, non-growth businesses also can be a source of wealth building. But it's also associated with more personal risk than employment with a large company.
- It's important that you seek long-term employment with organizations that value your participation in ownership, whether they are public or private.

Unwritten Rules – Dealing With Adversity

As I reflect on experience in business—particularly compared to school and other activities prior to entering business—I find the most surprising characteristic is also the most obvious: Work is hard.

Constant and ongoing, work requires a never-ending effort as long as you're able to participate. It will continue long after you're gone, energized by successive generations of eager participants enduring similar cycles of pain and gain. Work stands as an integral part of humanity. In business, it's an honorable path for dedicating a significant portion of creative energy to your personal sustenance, individual betterment, family support, and societal improvement.

Work in business seems to grow more difficult as the responsibility level increases. It's not that high-level jobs demand more physically, because they often don't. However, the responsibility for results inherent in high-level business leadership roles creates demanding and wearing pressure; and it never goes away. You frequently hear reference to desirable work that you can "leave at the office." You will not find this true of professional business careers. The problem becomes much worse if you're fortunate enough to advance in business, assuming responsibility for performance results, eventually judged by the investors. To accomplish results at this level, you will have to work through other people, in effect assuming responsibility for what they accomplish. Working in business is not all about you; it is all about the collective work and demonstrated results of a group of people.

The work of business is also hard because it inevitably involves artfully balancing competing priorities. In much of our business, that balancing act becomes the work: dealing with the competing interests of investors, customers, and employees. Investors' demand for a return remains hindered by the demand to do more for customers, which pressures your ability to incent and reward employees. This balancing cycle repeats every day, at both a strategic and tactical level, as we try to manage our resources to solve customers' problems and satisfy investors. One right answer never exists to any dilemma. There's always a way to improve on our results.

Most business mistakes arise from the ineffective balance of competing priorities, frequently due to communication problems. When problems become serious—affecting customers' expectations or ability to perform their business— mistakes can easily threaten a business's performance and reputation, and consequently employees' livelihoods. Situations with some degree of serious threat are common, as is risking significant loss from actions and decisions. Good business people learn to live with these risks. They're able to function effectively under this constant pressure.

I also observe a "normal" level of serious risk and exposure in day-to-day management of issues. And there are grave issues: potential business- and career-ending problems that are less frequent, but inevitable. These grave issues demand immediate attention, and result in company-changing actions. Invariably, when companies face these dramatic actions—cost control, layoff, divestiture, or restructuring—the cause is management neglect of a series of successive smaller problems. In my experience, the most common of these failures include: (1) not paying enough attention to rising costs as revenue plateaus or falls; (2) not following a focused business strategy; (3) ignoring customers' changing needs by focusing on internal issues, and (4) ignoring the need to constantly monitor and refine business strategy. I have been guilty of all these business sins. Even worse, at times I've recognized them and done nothing about them.

Only executive management deals directly with serious problems of this magnitude, requiring immediate action. An executive's understanding of his or her company—that view from the top—is always distorted. Employees typically show top execs a good face. This can be even more distorted if executives think they understand everything important occurring in their company. With no exceptions, the people who best know what's important to a company are those who perform the work creating value. They possess ideas, when understood and acted upon, that can benefit the business. It's every employee's job to look for signs of problems, try to understand them, and communicate these opinions upward. Good organizations will listen. They will also communicate downward to encourage open dialog and share ideas before they become policy. Those businesses that do not will eventually suffer hardship.

Acxiom Inc.'s long-term, former CEO Charles Morgan communicated directly to all employees in a weekly e-mail. While I doubt Charles wrote every word, the messages appeared open, obviously containing his thoughts and opinions. At the end of every message, he solicited comments, ideas and opinions from all employees. He also responded to these messages through an infrastructure that handled them; but I have no doubt he saw most of them and understood the messages delivered. This is a 5,000-employee company, and that effort consumed a significant amount of resources. It was really just a higher-tech suggestion box with two-way communication, but it proved an effective tool.

Early in 2001, Acxiom began to experience flattening sales. It appeared we were headed toward a serious hit to profitability. Like all of my employers, we waited longer than we should have to act. It eventually became apparent we had to implement cost controls, including reducing staff to match expense with revenue. Over a four-week period, we dealt with how to define and implement the changes required, and how to minimize the effect on our customers and employees. During those four weeks, Charles sent out 11 emails to all workers. He explained that we had problems, would have to address them, laid out our alternatives, and eventually confided our actions. In most companies, rank-and-file employees would only receive the layoffs announcement. In Acxiom, at least for this action, by the time we announced layoffs, the story was obvious and even old news. That's the best example I've seen of maintaining open communication through a crisis. The company weathered that particular storm with renewed strength.

In this Acxiom example, I do not want to misrepresent employees' attitude toward layoffs. In the circumstance I described, Acxiom management did about as much as it possibly could to prepare the workforce for the inevitable layoffs and salary controls; but this action was still poorly received. Employees spent a significant amount of time talking with each other about what could happen. Then, as any change took place, an intensive underground internal communications network summarized all the changes, particularly the layoffs, as soon as they occurred.

These kinds of non-productive, time-consuming internal discussions—what might happen, what's about to happen, what did happen, and what will happen next—are common in all companies. You should expect them as part of the process. When companies reach the financial stage where layoffs and severe cost reductions must occur, there is just no good way to do it. These actions are difficult because they hurt people, and many employees will be justifiably unhappy. You should not expect anything else. At best, the damage to morale and productivity will be short-lived; at worst, the company will never recover.

In most companies, when serious problems—those appearing to impact the company's ability to survive—begin to surface, most employees go into "protection" mode. In other words, they scramble to save themselves first, often at the expense of co-workers. Business crisis, like personal crisis, brings out the true character of a company and its employees. When a business is in trouble, you must pay serious attention to a plan of action, first to survive, and subsequently to improve. Focus is important, and the primary mission becomes protecting the business, not any particular individuals. This creates a difficult environment, and the actions required can become impersonal and harsh. This is when you clearly see that business life is not personal life. Decisions must be made for the good of the whole, and may be personally devastating.

Good business leaders separate themselves from their personal lives and feelings, and make decisions for the company's benefit. Good business leaders also do this with common sense and compassion for the people affected. To deal successfully with business leadership's financial requirements, particularly business crisis, and do it while exhibiting compassion represents another of management's difficult balancing acts. There is no single way to do this; but taking decisive action to benefit the business should be the primary objective. Doing the right thing for affected employees should guide the actions, but business survival must take priority.

After I had worked at Alcoa for about a year, I received the opportunity to go through a six-month metallurgist training program which included on-site visits to a number of Alcoa's plants. In one of those visits, to Davenport, Iowa, we met Ed Diefenbach, a legend among Alcoa's metallurgists. The architect of some of Alcoa's more sophisticated casting techniques, Ed was certainly an authority on aluminum production, and a good communicator. Our group of trainees consisted of aspiring career-types, wanting to get ahead as quickly as possible. We frequently asked our teachers and hosts, including Diefenbach, "How do you get ahead?" His position was not high-level, and we could not understand why someone so smart and knowledgeable remained an engineer, never becoming a manager. I will never forget what he told us. "Yeah, Alcoa wanted me to be a manager, and I tried it a while and did not care for it." When responding to the obvious question of "why" he said, "Well, they wanted me to fire my friends and I wouldn't do that." End of conversation.

At the time, I thought he just did not "have what it takes." I thought that I did and would not be held back. It seemed he just did not understand business or the commitment required. Needless to say, I believe differently now. At this stage in my career, I have much respect for Mr. Diefenbach and his principles. He made a decision about his business life based on his personal beliefs, and was willing to accept the consequences. He understood what Alcoa had to do and where he fit in, and was willing to only go as far as his beliefs would allow. I also respect Alcoa's decision to leave him out of the management track and focus him where he would be effective for the company. A company filled with "Diefenbachs" would fail, but companies that find a place for principled informal leaders like Ed Diefenbach should be admired.

My most difficult working experiences involved business crises when I held management responsibility. I have gone through the difficulty of declining profit, the implementation of poor products and services, lack of strategy, extreme cost control, laying off friends, and being laid off. Some of these problems occurred in every place I worked, and you should expect them as a normal course of business.

During these difficult times, you must understand the priority of business and protect the company first. This includes, in order, investors, customers and employees. But we all have to live with ourselves, within our families and communities. To do that well, you must be direct, open, honest, concerned, focused, and continually deliver your best effort while you try to do what intuitively seems right. This is business; but you also have to be a person.

Chapter Summary:

- The pressure of responsibility for results is inherent to high-level business leadership. It is demanding and wearing, and never goes away.
- Working in business is not all about you; it is all about the collective work and demonstrated results of a group of people.
- The work of business is also hard because it inevitably involves artfully balancing competing priorities.
- One right answer never exists to any dilemma. There's always a way to improve on our results.
- Most business mistakes result from the ineffective balance of competing priorities, frequently due to communication problems.
- Situations with some degree of serious threat are common, as is risking significant loss from actions and decisions. Good business people learn to live with these risks.
- The people who best know what's important to a company are those who perform the work creating value. They possess ideas, when understood and acted upon, that can benefit the business.
- When companies reach the financial stage where layoffs and severe cost reductions must occur, there is just no good way to do it. These actions are difficult because they hurt people, and many employees will be justifiably unhappy.

- When serious problems—those appearing to impact the company's ability to survive—begin to surface, most employees go into "protection" mode.
- Business crisis, like personal crisis, brings out the true character of a company and its employees.
- Good business leaders separate themselves from their personal lives and feelings to make decisions that benefit the company. Good business leaders also do this with common sense and compassion for the people affected.
- During these difficult times, you must understand the priority of business and protect the company first. This includes, in order, investors, customers and employees.
- You must be direct, open, honest, concerned, focused and continually deliver your best effort while you try to do what intuitively seems right.

The Bottom Line

Such an integral part of our lives, working factors into almost all of our experience. It consumes close to half our waking hours. It's our source of livelihood, allowing us to first survive, and also achieve many of our personal objectives. Even when not working, we are still close to it. Either we just left, prepare to go back, think about it, try to get away from it, or try to find it. Work can dominate our lives, so trying to "summarize" working in business is almost as difficult as summarizing life.

I prefer to summarize how we should *approach* work. You can apply some guidelines every day. Don Hatfield, one of my Systematics co-workers and an amateur philosopher, summarized our work-participation directive this way: Work hard, do right, have fun. I have since heard these same guidelines from other sources, but I always associate them with Don. They describe a simple approach with complex depth and meaning. Consider them your mantra for success.

Work Hard

As I reflect back, I'm not sure when I began believing that working hard is important. If anything, I suppose it came as a process of societal osmosis through my parents and the 1950s environment. My dad was a farmer. He left for work each day before I got up, came in around sundown, and labored over paperwork much of the time he was home. He obviously spent a lot of his time working. I assumed this was normal. I cannot recall him ever telling me I should work hard, but I know his example left a lot of "should" and "responsibility" messages influencing my work ethic.

My first job, during high school, was as a laborer for a farm implement distributor. I mostly cleaned the shop and performed some minor assembly. They hired me because my dad asked them to, though they didn't have much clearly defined work for me to do. At times I would run out of assignments, not knowing what to do next or how to find out. It seems stupid now, but I remember being extremely nervous if I wasn't actually doing something. I still feel that way, anxious and concerned if I don't have a clear sense of what job I need to perform. I become uncomfortable doing nothing. I do not assume that means I am a hard worker, just that I feel guilty if I'm not working. When I see something that needs doing, my first reaction is to quickly understand what's necessary, then immediately jump in and start.

I spent my early career years working in factories, developing great respect for people who carried out the hot, dirty, physically demanding work required in that business. I love to see how smart people approach difficult work, developing ways to minimize their effort and yet maximize productivity. My view of factory work slants toward the professional and managerial roles. So I have a difficult time understanding and accepting the traditional view of labor in labor versus management issues.

The summer after my junior year in engineering school, I worked as a trainee in an Arkansas aluminum reduction plant's casting department. This particular facility included a casting laboratory, run by the plant metallurgist. An ideal training job, it primarily involved quality control; but we also performed our own alloying and casting in a pilot foundry. I was able to work directly with a variety of processes. With sand casting machinery, we made our own molds for alloy testing. One day, the sand conveyor jammed. Thinking nothing about it, I grabbed a wrench and started taking off a large sidepiece to free up the conveyor. I noticed a couple of guys from the plant standing in the door, staring at me. They looked like they wanted to fight, so I asked if I could help them. One of them snapped, "What do you think you're doing?" "Fixing this conveyor," I said. He quickly replied, "No you're not. You're cutting our throats with that wrench!" Then they walked away.

I was baffled. I had no idea what they were talking about. That was my first direct exposure to unions and the contractual work separation between management and labor. My repair job resulted in a grievance, a problem for the plant metallurgist. I considered the whole affair nutty. I am now sure the grievance was legitimate based on the union agreement; but I continue to hold a low opinion of artificial labor divisions based on rank or contracts. This small incident represents one of many that shaped my opinion of work environments' value. I favor those that foster participation of equally contributing team members, and I oppose the waste of internal business squabbling over who alone controls each job function.

That's one of the qualities that attract me to technology-based businesses: the absence of unions and labor contracts, with all employees willingly participating to get the job done. I become energized by pitching in with others to complete a task, and continue to marvel at groups who distribute assignments to capable workers, naturally improving efficiency. I know everyone does not work under the same set of business behavior rules. There are hard workers and slackers in all forms of work, in all types of businesses, and at all levels. But I am sold on hard, concentrated work, dedicated to accomplish an end result that benefits a company. That's the best way to direct your working life.

No doubt, all work involves some difficult elements and can be considered "hard," at least when done well. While I understood the physical intensity and production demands of manufacturing, I was surprised at the mental effort, time demands and continuing stress of information-technology tasks. Much of IT work tends to be project-oriented and therefore cyclical. In the early stages, with the deadline far in the future, you can expect a normal eight- to nine-hour day. But as deadlines near, and the project typically falls behind schedule, time and stress demands become intense. I've seen many projects where team members worked long periods without sleep, labored through many successive weekends, making an incredible effort to complete the commitments. We would blame that intensity on poor project planning and management, but the end result was always similar. You can commonly expect this: the task is to get the job done, whatever the effort required.

On the other hand, you must take care not to worship long hours and intense effort as work's essence or the measure of a good worker.

Beware of managers who speak reverently of the long hours they put in, or their staff puts in, as a not-so-subtle de facto standard for acceptance into the company or team. You don't have to kill yourself to succeed in business. A management team that directs a company in this manner is trying to help only themselves and not their company.

In bank operations' information technology, one of the more difficult clerical/support tasks involves reconciling transactions. Obviously, banks find it highly important to be accurate to the penny. They all face requirements to assemble, read, and distribute large numbers of financial transactions daily. Each day, a large volume of the transaction count comes from checks read by fascinating high-speed reader/sorter machines. These devices read the MICR line of all checks, store the detail and totals, and sort the checks for further distribution. They document what they read and verify/prove the totals. Of course, the machines aren't perfect, and reading errors must be identified, reconciled and corrected in a time pressure-cooker environment.

In the late 1970s when I worked with Pontiac State Bank in Michigan for Systematics, we converted the bank to our item-capturing and reconcilement software. We had taken over the bank's IT staff, and as a result, they were most of our employees. This work required strict time pressure, with financial consequences for the bank if not completed on time and well. One reconcilement clerk, I cannot remember her name, proved fast and smart in adapting to the new system, becoming an informal staff leader. We promoted her to a supervisory position. She did quite well, taking on additional responsibilities. I believed she had the intelligence, communication skills, motivation and business sense to assume higher-level management positions. One day, in a complete surprise to me, she resigned to work on the assembly line at General Motors Truck and Coach. Her new job: to screw parts into truck cabs, shift work at the starting hourly wage. The new job offered significantly more money than we could pay. So she had a financial reason we couldn't match in the short-term; but her logic for the change is what startled me.

As she explained, "If you get on with the plants, you got it made. My Daddy told me all you have to do is put in your 90 days (a phrase meaning "stay through the probationary period and get into the union"), and then you just have to act like you are working!" Think about that. Here is a person whose father had taught her it was acceptable, even desirable, to work for a company, get paid, and only *act* like you were working. That just floors me. Why would you want to do that? Do you think a company/job where people only act like they are working has any chance of surviving? How long will you keep that job before being laid off? How could you live with yourself? And this is what your parents told you?

When I say "work hard" at your job, I mean just the opposite from the parental direction described in this story. I mean do your best, to the fullest extent of your ability, every day you're there. Do everything you can to make your company successful. Put the company and your co-workers first. If you do, you will likely become more successful at work than the person I described. For sure, you'll be able to live with yourself, satisfied that you did your best. That is all you, or anyone else, should ask.

Do Right

In the 1978 Orange Bowl, my beloved Arkansas Razorbacks were playing Oklahoma, then ranked number two in the national polls. I don't recall whether Arkansas was ranked at the time, but they were certainly a major underdog. To make matters worse, Arkansas coach Lou Holtz suspended three starters the day before the team made the trip to Miami. So not only was Arkansas supposed to lose, sportswriters and fans predicted the game to be a rout. Earlier in the day on January 1, number one Texas lost its bowl game, so an Oklahoma win would have made them the nation's top team. As it turned out the game was a rout. Only Arkansas won that day, 31-6 in one of the most memorable games in Razorback history.

Holtz's only explanation for why he suspended the three players: They broke the "do-right" rule. It was never clear what they did, and the media and fans were ready to string Holtz up before the game. Since they won in such dramatic fashion, the do-right rule became forever immortalized for the Arkansas sports fan.

That may be the first time I heard the term, but not the last time by any means. When faced with a business decision, by far the most common question I've heard asked—and now the most common question I ask—is, "What's the right thing to do in this situation?" It's a simple question with incredible depth. Frequently the right answer is what your gut instinct tells you. You must take all affected parties and circumstances into account including customers, employees, shareholders, long- and short-term impact, strategy consistency, and impact on business survival.

Please note that I did not ask, "How does it affect my career?" That's not how you make business decisions. Still, I've been amazed over the years at how many people do just that.

How do you gain a sense for what is right? Who sets the guidelines or rules for being right?

I think an unwritten code of business behavior exists. Let's call it business morals, primarily taught by example, clarifying what is right. Business ethics strongly influence business morals, which are not the same as personal or religious morals. The number one code of business morals states that you do not lie, cheat or steal. You also honor your commitments, those contractual, but also those of your word. You place high priority on your relationship with customers, and must respond to what they believe, not just what you think you told them. You are obligated to communicate clearly and fairly. If you don't know an answer or how to respond, you should make that clear and explain why. You have a right to make a profit, and should not be ashamed or try to hide that from your customers.

Business morals center on the company and doing what's right for the company. You should prioritize the company over individuals, and company survival is unfortunately more important than personal survival. Competitors, those that would choose to go after the same business as your company, definitely are the enemy. No one expects you to be kind to them, and you should aggressively try to defeat them. But you also should treat competitors with respect. *Never* go against business morals in your competitive actions.

In 1982, due to the enduring perseverance of a senior salesperson, Systematics developed the opportunity to sell its onsite facilities-management services to a New York bank. In today's language, this deal's potential impact on the company was huge. The relationship would bring more than twice the revenue of any existing Systematics account. New York banks were respected throughout the world for their industry leadership; and none had turned over their data processing responsibility to a company such as ours. In that respect, this deal offered the promise of a home-run competitive win in addition to its significant financial impact.

Our sales team had completed negotiations for a five-year contract, intense negotiations to say the least. We were beginning to plan implementation, working with existing employees in other locations, preparing for them to move to New York and take on this sizable challenge. The company was excited!

The only remaining formality to finalize the deal involved a meeting between our chairman, Walter Smiley, and the bank's chairman, Edmund Safra. An internationally acclaimed banker from Geneva, Switzerland, Mr. Safra actually owned this bank. He was reported to be one of the richest men in the world. The meeting was held at the New York bank in Mr. Safra's private quarters. It quickly became intense. In a surprise move, Mr. Safra continued negotiating, insisting on the right to terminate the agreement at any time without cause.

These facilities-management agreements were complex and somewhat unique for each customer. But in all cases with Systematics, we committed to install a complete set of banking application software; modify, enhance and support it over time; revise and maintain the mainframe computing hardware required; and provide a knowledgeable staff to support the bank's implementation and use of these new systems for an extended time period. The relationship involved dedicating existing Systematics employees to the bank client; moving some of them to the client's offices; hiring the existing bank data-processing department, and financing hardware.

One of the keys to Systematics' success had been its strict adherence to a financial model. This model provided a reasonably secure long-term revenue stream, financing for capital expenditures, employee career progression, and funding to enhance its product offerings. In Walter Smiley and the company's opinion, agreements allowing its customers to exit-at-will—in effect making the contracts short-term—would not protect the investments required to properly manage the business. In simpler terms, the pacts would not be "right" for the company as we had chosen to run it.

Of course Mr. Safra realized his bank's business represented a significant opportunity and increased responsibility for Systematics. He was trying to use that leverage to negotiate favorable terms, and to assure a way out of the agreement if the relationship soured. Walter was taken aback by this unexpected approach; and he took a resistant stance because Mr. Safra wanted him to change one of our core business-management principles.

While the discussions remained professional and cordial, they were quite serious. Walter didn't agree to the provisions requested. He explained that we had built our company on the belief that funding from guaranteed long-term contracts allowed us to offer true careers to our employees, continual product improvement investment for our clients, as well as reasonable pricing. He stressed that a contract with exit-at-will provisions would violate those principles, making it impossible to manage the company in the manner we believed had made us successful. We were making a long-term commitment, and our model only worked if our clients made a similar commitment.

After a weekend of agonizing with the Systematics team over this large relationship's potential benefits, Walter led us to our choice: We would walk away on principle. I was involved in those discussions, and remember the agony of being so close to an industry-leading deal; but we all shared a good feeling. We knew we had tried hard, but just could not abandon such an important principle. It felt like a failure, but we knew we had done the right thing!

In this case, Walter's insistence on principle in his conversations with Mr. Safra brought an unexpected conclusion. A few days after we walked away from the deal, he called Walter back and accepted our terms. His comment to Walter: He admired a company that would sacrifice a clear opportunity on the principle of "doing the right thing." That was the kind of company he wanted to do business with.

The resulting relationship became the longest and most profitable in Systematics history. To this day, I am proud of the position we took. It was honestly all we could do. It wasn't gamesmanship or politics, and left us truly "feeling" that we had done our best. I also had the highest respect for Mr. Safra and his bank, and am honored to have worked as their partner.

I submit that you can learn the right business thing to do by paying attention to how it "feels." It's not automatic. It's a behavior you learn, and trial and error will help you improve over time. You should lead your decision-making by what is best for the business. I have found that, in most all cases, that kind of thinking will also lead to what is right for you. I believe businesses led in this manner become the best ones. In the long run, however, we all have to live with ourselves. At some point, you may be faced with decisions that make you uncomfortable personally. In those cases you have to do what is right for you. Your "feeling" will become your most important guide.

Since businesses, even small businesses, require the interaction of a number of people, you must accept the inevitability of politics as an influence. Frequently, organizational politics are criticized as an extreme negative, to be avoided if at all possible. In this context, politics—better described as business politics—consists of businesspeople using friendships, relationships, rumor, innuendo, and other forms of indirect and informal communication to gain individual advantage. You should approach business with the understanding that politics is a given, even the natural order, and neither good nor bad. Impossible to avoid, it's just a part of group dynamics we all must deal with.

Because of this, I believe understanding and even "working" organizational politics is a critical survival skill, to be learned as a process. Knowing the people with both formal and informal power, communicating in all directions at the appropriate time, documenting intentions and actions, paying attention to issues that might personally affect others, and being concerned and considerate about co-workers are all political actions entirely appropriate in business. Like a lot of business, a fine line of judgment can exist between good politics and obvious brown-nosing, insincere concern, or flattery.

The best business leaders possess a genuine concern for their business, their customers, employees, and investors. For some, this is natural behavior. If true caring for your business constituents' welfare isn't normal and natural for you, spend some effort putting yourself in their shoes. Understand your business from their point of view: what matters to them and why. More than likely, this understanding will lead to empathy, which your fellow workers and customers will appreciate. Your false concern for others becomes easily transparent, and despised by everyone around you. Do the right thing. And work hard to understand what is right.

Have Fun

As I approach the end of my business career (let's say it's the last third, okay?), it's easy to say in a meaningful way, "Life is too short. If you are going to spend most of your life's best years working, at least make sure you have fun."

I am serious about this. I don't mean that work should constantly be a good time and entertain you; but you should be able to look back and sincerely say, "I'm glad I did that. I feel good about my work, and I've enjoyed the results and the relationships of my effort." I know this is important and true today, but I can't say I knew that early on.

Before I started working, I pictured it as serious and a responsibility. I was to put out my best effort, do what I was asked to do, and strive to advance. I expected to be promoted to positions of power and influence, assume greater responsibilities, always working toward the opportunity to be "in charge." I expected to make enough money to support myself, my family, and live comfortably. Having fun was not a goal. But I sure have had fun.

Here are the keys for making work fun: (1) evolve towards work that you consider valuable; (2) make it worthy of your time, and (3) work around people you respect and enjoy. This is easy to say, but it's difficult to manage over time. Your preparation for work, which in most cases includes some amount of education and training, is incomplete preparation at best. Even with the best of research about a new work environment, you will be learning at the start. You will learn what you're supposed to do and what's required for business and personal success. You will also learn what's important to you and what you enjoy. You should expect your interests, motivation and pleasure to change over the course of your working lifetime. I don't believe all people will make these changes in a similar fashion, but I am convinced all people will go through significant change.

The first requirement for having fun at work: Seek your passion and motivation in a work setting, and go after it. If you're pleased by what your company does, and by your individual effort and contribution, you can have fun. If you don't believe in the value of your company's work, and cannot see results from your own contribution, it's doubtful that work will ever become fun.

I also believe you must like and respect the people you work with. As I have discussed in previous chapters, your co-workers do not have to be personal friends; in fact, that is a problem. It can be fun to work with people who are knowledgeable, respectful, reliable, honest, trustworthy, willing to teach, willing to learn and team players. These will be your business friends, people you spend much of your life with. While you are working together, for some kind of common purpose, they will remain close.

You should stay aware that business conditions can, and will, change the interrelationship of business friends. Don't be surprised when someone with whom you worked closely, with whom you felt a bond, drifts away as a business friend when business conditions separate you. Changing business will change your business friendships. Business reasons, not personal ones, drive these changes.

One of the most effective ways to have fun at work involves possessing a sense of humor. Some of my least favorite co-workers have been those that took themselves too seriously. I have repeated the mantra, "It's not personal, it is just business." In the same manner, we can also say, "This is not life, it is just work!" Work is part of your life, not all of it. People with no personal interests outside their working lives become narrow, uninteresting, unhealthy, and certainly no fun to be around. The same can be said of those who take themselves too seriously.

Learn to laugh at yourself and what you do. Make it clear to others that you are willing to do so. The people you work with will appreciate it, respect you, and want to be around you. More than likely, they already know you are strange—most of us are—and showing that you understand will place you in agreement with them.

Work should be fun, but not your only source of fun. The healthy life is well balanced among personal relationships, family, physical health, spiritual well-being, and work. Though difficult, juggling these important factors with an artful balance optimizes your contribution to society and your ability to live a productive, healthy life.

It is your most important job.

Chapter Summary:

- There are hard workers and slackers in all forms of work, in all types of businesses, and at all levels. I am sold on hard, concentrated work, dedicated to accomplish an end result that benefits a company. That's the best way to direct your working life.
- You must take care not to worship long hours and intense effort as the essence of work or the measure of a good worker.
- You do not have to kill yourself to succeed in business. A management team that directs a company in this manner is trying to help only themselves and not their company.
- Do your best, to the fullest extent of your ability, every day you are there. Do everything you can to make your company successful. Put the company and your co-workers first.
- When faced with a decision about business, by far the most common question I have heard asked—and now the most common question I ask—is, "What's the right thing to do in this situation?"
- Business ethics strongly influence business morals, which are not the same as personal or religious morals. The number one code of business morals states that you do not lie, cheat or steal. You also honor your commitments, those contractual, but also those of your word.
- Business morals center around the company and doing what is right for the company. You should prioritize the company over individuals. Company survival is unfortunately more important than personal survival.

- We all have to live with ourselves, and at some point you may be faced with decisions that make you uncomfortable personally. In those cases, you have to do what is right for you. Your "feeling" will become your most important guide.
- Business politics consists of businesspeople using friendships, relationships, rumor, innuendo, and other forms of indirect and informal communication to gain individual advantage.
- I believe understanding and even "working" organizational politics is a critical survival skill, to be learned as a process.
- The best business leaders possess a genuine concern for their business, their customers, employees, and investors.
- Your false concern for others becomes easily transparent, and despised by everyone around you.
- Here are the keys for making work fun: (1) evolve towards work that you consider valuable; (2) make it worthy of your time, and (3) work around people you respect and enjoy.
- You should expect your interests, motivation and pleasure to change over the course of your working lifetime.
- Changing business will alter your business friendships. Business reasons, not personal ones, drive these changes.
- One of the most effective ways to have fun at work is to possess a sense of humor.
- Learn to laugh at yourself and what you do, and make it clear to others that you are willing to do so. The people you work with will appreciate it, respect you, and want to be around you.
- The healthy life is well balanced among personal relationships, family, physical health, spiritual well being, and work.

Appendix 1 – Who Am I?

You may have read this book with some important questions in mind: Who is this guy? Where does he come from? What does he know about business? Why should I care what he thinks?

This Appendix is a personal discussion of my career. In a similar manner to the previous Chapter Summaries, I have highlighted learning experiences and insights. These statements confirm something I took to heart from that particular career stage. I consider them relevant and important to someone starting out.

I was born in 1946, the first year of the baby boom, and grew up in a typical 1950s environment—small Southern town, neighborhood schools, working father, and stay-at-home mother. I was no jock, but thankfully made good grades, and was particularly competent in math and science. As a result of high-school aptitude testing, I went to an engineering undergraduate program, desiring to do the best I could and become successful. Whatever that meant. Society was dominated by the Cold War, and the ongoing race for technological superiority. Many aspiring professionals wandered to engineering, even though most of us, me included, had no clue about engineers' roles and responsibilities.

Upon graduating from Vanderbilt University with a mechanical-engineering degree, I went to work for Alcoa as an ingot metallurgist at a North Carolina casting plant. Like all my work experience, this became a great learning opportunity. Most importantly, I discovered I did not want to be an engineer! It became obvious that the good engineers were amazingly creative. At best I am a creative hack. I'm really attentive to detail and follow instructions well; but I couldn't see betting my career on my ability to deliver technical innovation.

After just a few months, I became aware that the people who were promoted the fastest, acquired the most power, and earned the most money were the plant managers. So I targeted that position. I deselected myself from the engineering discipline and into one that seemed more appropriate for me.

But I was working with "feelings," not rational thought and objective measurement. As I look back, it's apparent I wasn't concerned about job stability. I was looking to make more money and gain more responsibility, as quickly as I could make it happen.

> Today I would argue that the best early career goal is *not* to push immediately for the most money and the most responsibility. I believe in developing a strategy, planning for your career to evolve over a long term (30+ years). At the time I targeted management, I was looking at immediate salary and my next position, assuming everything else would work out for the best. Today I would encourage a more thorough examination of your personal goals, capabilities and shortcomings. Also, plan to select good employers, work on your deficiencies, and gain broad experience. That's not the path I chose, but my experience tells me that's what *you* should do.

I was convinced that the fastest path to management was through more education, specifically a master's degree in business administration (MBA). Again, I did not have a clear picture of MBA school; I was just trying to speed up my corporate ladder climb. I chose to attend the Krannert School of Management at Purdue University, a program with MBA-like curriculum designed for science majors and engineers with no business-school background. The school offered a Master of Science in Industrial Administration (MSIA), a program completed in one calendar year. In just 12 months I would be back at work, with money flowing in, not out. I chose Purdue because a Vanderbilt classmate I respected went there the year before. I did not even apply to any other school.

> As I look back on most of my life's major decisions, I now see the circumstantial way I approached them, and the powerful influence of other people, particularly friends, on my thinking. I don't consider this good or bad, but it certainly points out the importance of choosing friends wisely, seeking good advice from people you respect, and being well grounded with a clear sense of your own goals.

The Purdue curriculum included a significant appreciation of entrepreneurs. Students typically took the role of company executive. We actually began to believe we were qualified to lead organizations, infecting me with the typical MBA disease of "wanting to run my own business!" Like many MBAs, I needed some experience-based education to eventually learn what I could not do, and that in business we rarely do anything on our own.

After Purdue, I accepted a position with Air Products and Chemicals of Trexlertown, Pennsylvania, quickly moving into a position of product manager for a line of welding equipment. While I could have gone back to the aluminum business on an eventual management track, I chose the highest pay and a more immediate chance for management responsibility.

> Air Products was, and remains, an excellent company. But I eventually began to understand that, no matter what any organization implies (or what you hear) in its promotion/recruiting, you must take certain actions before you become a key player in any business. You must invest a certain amount of time in learning the business, your own capabilities, and how to make a contribution. That's how you establish a positive reputation.

My broad, fast-moving experience with Air Products gave me an excellent opportunity to learn. Today I believe the knowledge you bring to a position in your early career isn't nearly as important as your learning skills. But I did maintain a certain degree of technical competence for the first seven years of my career, and that was important to me at the time.

Through my mentor George Metterhauser's introduction, I met some young guys who had started a small business with Air Products' equipment, and they became my heroes. This was my "run your own business" desire coming out. With a lot of their help, I created a business plan to replicate their operation in another market area, the South, closer to home. The quest for funding was much more difficult than I imagined.

Eventually I found a willing partner in Ben Pearson Manufacturing Company from my hometown, Pine Bluff, Arkansas. They desired to develop a service business to support their farm implement manufacturing business. I altered my business plan just enough to accommodate them. At age 26, I quit Air Products to start Metal Services, Inc. in Pine Bluff, supplying heat treating, chrome plating, and steel shape cutting to manufacturing businesses in the mid-South market. Today, this seems like a high-risk decision. I had a promising job with a successful company, had recently bought a home, and our first child was a year old. At the time, I saw it as just another career step, and I had complete confidence we would succeed!

My initial customer was my partner, Ben Pearson Manufacturing, and the three-year goal was to at least replicate their revenue contribution through outside business development. Again, as I look back on my career, I am amazed that we started this business. It is astounding that these partners and bankers trusted me to run it, and that I was crazy enough to take this risk, uproot my family, and start from nothing in a field I knew little about. I can also now see that my enthusiasm to start a small business and be "in charge" caused me to overlook some obvious problems that eventually made success impossible.

The mid-1970s energy crisis and its subsequent impact on small geographic-based manufacturing services and the farm implement business did us in. The loss of volume from our primary customer and severe price competition from other service suppliers ended this business after three years. This proved a great learning experience for me. But, in the final analysis, ours was like many a small business: it never should have been started.

Faced with the prospect of not only no career, but also no job, I began calling everyone I knew looking for alternatives. I had a few requirements based on this recent experience. The company must be sound enough to provide regular paychecks that did not bounce, and it could not be a family-owned business. I needed a business with some inherent growth and an appetite for young, eager, aspiring management professionals.

Through the contact of a friend, I was able to convince Systematics, Inc., a Little Rock based computer company, to hire me. The positives of my employment with Systematics are the root of most of my business success. I will be forever grateful to my friend Dudley Shollmier who brought me in, and to CEO Walter Smiley who ran the risk of hiring me.

> The most important lesson from this phase of my career evolution is the all-important value of personal contacts and networking. This may not be what you want to hear, but most job selections derive from (1) who you know, (2) your reputation, and (3) your qualifications. Your most important job search preparation can therefore be a wide network of contacts and friends, and *their* networks of contacts and friends.

I have seen important job selection decisions influenced by relationships gained from school, church, sports (particularly golf), fraternities and sororities, hometowns, community service activities, and of course, families. I advocate a shameless use of contacts to obtain interviews and consideration for jobs. These connections will not guarantee that you can keep a job, but they can make it possible for you to find one.

As I look back on the early years of Systematics, it was a conservatively led, focused business with a competitive product, outstanding market vision, a sound business model, and superior leaders—clear ingredients for success. But this wasn't so clear to me at the time. I had no idea where this employment would lead. It appeared to be a growing company in an interesting, new field. Its leaders were young, and it was even based near my hometown. At that time, this was enough for my commitment.

Systematics sold its services across the United States. The facilities management approach meant that well over 50% of its leaders and key employees must live in remote locations, working with acquired staff to deliver services under long-term contracts. I was eager to learn, grow and contribute, so I volunteered to go anywhere and do anything. I meant it. An added bonus: Even if I had to move, at some time later I could return to Systematics' corporate office in Little Rock, closer to my hometown. At that time in my career, I thought of the moving obligation as merely an irritant, something that would inconvenience my family and me for a while as we adapted to a different area, home and lifestyle, but certainly not something I should avoid.

After learning as much as possible through the next six months, I moved into a management position over a small, Pine Bluff-based Systematics data center with multiple clients. Later in that first year of employment, I moved to a much more important position, taking over a new client relationship/data center for a relatively large account. These were the company's key operational jobs. Having this opportunity after only a year represented a significant challenge. I considered it an honor.

The client, however, was in Pontiac, Michigan, which meant a move to Detroit. Since I committed to move anywhere, relocating to Detroit was only a minor annoyance. But I miscalculated the damaging effects this move placed on my marriage and family. I didn't understand it at the time, but making this move became one of the most personally selfish decisions of my career.

If I had not accepted this assignment, another would have come along in a few months, likely in a more desirable location for us. While moving again was a given at that stage in my Systematics career, I should have involved my family more in the overall decision. The affect on my career progression would probably have been minimal, but the positive impact on my family would have been worth it.

Today, I would advise anyone in similar circumstances to engage in serious family goal setting and negotiation before making this kind of change. I also see a significant difference in families today, particularly on the subject of moving. Today's spousal relationships seem to involve both parties more actively and openly in these decisions, and I believe that's healthy. The sound advice: Do not uproot your family unless you all are convinced it's the right thing to do. Negotiate fairly with each other, and be clear with your employer about what you will and will not do. In the long run, this approach will be best for your personal satisfaction.

I served as the on-site manager at the Pontiac location. I'll confess I was still very green, with much to learn about how to lead. I have later come to understand the poor work attitude of the site's acquired staff. These were, for the most part, professional employees. But the strong trade union influence and predominant "us vs. them" working atmosphere created difficult obstacles. You can overcome these kinds of attitude and performance problems with a combination of (1) direct, open, and truthful communication, (2) consistent and clear policies, and (3) fair and equal treatment. Employee attitude and performance problems are not the result of trade unions, although an alignment of workers against the company's overall interests is problematic and frequently associated with unions.

If you have a choice between a company with obvious attitudinal or cultural biases against management and one already with an alignment between employee objectives and company objectives, choose the one where this hard management-employee work has already occurred.

Pontiac was my baptism under fire into the world of complex information-technology conversion projects. We made many mistakes, working with under-supported software and employees with limited skill (not to mention my limited skill as their leader). The operational processing of banks is time- and quality-sensitive, with little room for error as problems can threaten a bank's ability to open its doors. We eventually completed these conversions, but only through the brute force of time expended by a small, dedicated staff backed up by a knowledgeable corporate staff in the home office.

During the heat of conversion activity, the data entry operators presented me with a list of demands, similar to threatening a strike. Data entry required considerable skill, and good operators were hard to find. While commonly among Systematics' lowest paid positions, our Detroit operators were some of the highest paid because of the wage competition in this heavily industrial city. However, our wage rates were significantly less than those of the automotive plants, and we did not believe we could compete with them. I immediately feared the entire group would quit over wages, and we couldn't replace them. I also didn't understand their concerns. I agreed to meet with them for a series of both collective and individual sessions.

As it turned out, their issues were not compensation related except for a couple of inequities. Their main problems were scheduling, workload management, internal communications, and relations with other departments. We were able to fix these problems by increasing the frequency of communication, being open with each other, and reacting flexibly to their need for scheduling and workload management changes. In that employment market, the only way they knew to make themselves heard was presenting a list of demands. As a result of this crisis, I think we all learned a lot about the value of ongoing, open communication.

After two years on-site in Pontiac, we completed the conversions nearly on schedule, close enough to be considered a success. My reward: the opportunity to do it again, with a larger bank in Wichita, Kansas.

The Wichita assignment involved the same changeover of software and hardware, but much more complex. The larger bank actually performed processing services for a number of small banks. In addition, we were called in to replace one of our competitors who had failed. That meant we had to overcome the client's recent bad taste for facilities management. We succeeded, completing all conversions on time and within budget.

Systematics had never accomplished this many conversions for a client over such a short time period. This became one of my greatest personal work triumphs. In Wichita for three years, I built some of the best business relationships I have ever experienced, both with customers and our own employees.

I have always admired people who set goals. I have almost always eyed some work-related target. But I never maintained the discipline to set a series of goals, work for them, modify them, accomplish them, and then set more.

However, over my 35-year span of working, I can remember clearly setting one business goal—becoming a Systematics district manager. District managers were the bosses from the corporate office, and I saw their job as a great blend of corporate leadership, customer relations and field operations. They possessed ultimate responsibility for executing many complex customer contractual relationships, and were expected to generate profitable growth.

I reached this goal in my next assignment after Wichita, and was able to move my family to Little Rock, close to our original home. As a district manager, I assumed the responsibility for three data-center locations, initially all in Kansas. In this position, I was assigned to work with our clients' executive management in accomplishing the primary objective—perpetually maintaining these large-facilities management relationships. Reaching this position after only five years—in an industry I knew nothing about until I joined—proved a major milestone. I am as proud of that today as when it happened. But I also know it was possible due to many other people's efforts, in no way just my own.

Working with bankers and "data processing" personnel, I received a serious taste of another professional milestone: assuming responsibility for something I didn't know how to do. As an engineer and product manager—even as creator of Metal Services, Inc.—I always proved technically competent regarding our responsibilities. In fact, I actually played the expert role for much of this work. Moving into bank data processing, I observed three major differences when compared to my previous experience in manufacturing:

1. The work environment was not only clean, but sterile;

2. The technical experts were very young and bright, but not experienced with business;

3. The work was intense and, frankly, extremely hard.

My success was determined by the work and success of others. Since I didn't have a clue how to perform the work, I quickly adopted a collaborative or coaching management style. It was comfortable for me and matched what little management training I had received. But I became this type of manager out of necessity. Nothing else would work.

I then advanced to executive management. At Systematics, we had an executive committee reporting to the CEO. I joined that committee in 1983 as an operational manager, supervising our data centers in the United States' eastern half. Responsible for post-sale execution and maintaining our long-term contractual agreements, I focused on client relations and managing our rather large group of employees.

I moved in and out of similar positions for the next 14 years, in varying geographies and with different responsibilities for operational, corporate and sales functions. I continued as a member of the executive committee, over that time seeing changes in CEOs, market emphasis, profitability, growth, and even company ownership. These led to serious business cultural and political challenges, and surviving them remains a major accomplishment.

New leadership and ownership challenged the long-term viability of Systematics' business model, partly out of healthy new perspectives as well as out of ignorance. I frequently addressed initiatives to change our products, marketing, sales, customer relations, reporting, compensation, contracts, and most all our business strategy's components. Each required challenging the status quo, when we should alter direction, and when we should resist change. I became quite good at deciding when to remain flexible and when to fight.

In the time I worked there, Systematics grew from less than $9 million in annual revenue to almost $1 billion. The company saw success, failure, and established itself as a market leader, predominantly supplying a narrow segment of the high-technology service industry. I was in the right place at the right time, with a solid growth company in a growth market. I collaborated with an outstanding team of managers and employees, and enjoyed the company's cultural bias to reward its employees through sharing in ownership. I was able to witness and participate at a level higher than I ever could have conceived when I began my career as an engineer.

In my remaining 14 years with Systematics, I moved responsibilities from the Eastern United States to the West, allowing me to work individually with most of our clients. In addition, when we reduced our executive committee to three members in 1987, for two years I managed all non-operations functions. In that capacity, I led systems development, human resources, training, finance and legal, including investor relations. I don't claim to have been great with any of these. But we did continue to grow, and I was fortunate to have direct exposure to most every facet of the organization. I had so much to learn.

In 1988, our primary owner Stephens, Inc. brought in a new CEO to replace the founder. The new leader was a career IBM executive with a sales background. The conventional wisdom implied his task was to grow the company more rapidly. The former CEO remained briefly as chairman, but the new guy was clearly brought in to take over. These two could not co-exist in leadership for long.

The new CEO's initial impact was on target with Stephens' expectations, as he was able to ramp up the growth. This growth soon attracted a suitor, Alltel Corporation, a rural telephone and wireless company, also based in Little Rock. Since the political and business connections between Alltel and Stephens were close, I now assume this acquisition was part of Stephens' overall plan. It certainly was a "home run" financial transaction. The net result: Stephens' was able to change their holdings from 49% of Systematics to 10% of Alltel, realizing more than a $300 million gain. This was risk mitigation for them, as well as for other Systematics shareholders, like me!

Our CEO was effective when he assumed leadership of Systematics. But he eventually started a series of changes that led to the company's demise as a growth engine. I believe our new leader did not grasp the subtleties before he began to take action. As a result, his changes created turmoil. Primarily, this happened when he brought in many of his former IBM business associates, assigning them leadership positions. Their integration into Systematics was painful. We took our eye off strategy, the market, our competition, and customer needs as we fought internally to adapt to these new players and, frankly, teach them how to run the business. The CEO also led us into questionable sales transactions that enhanced revenue but were difficult to make profitable. His growth commitments to Alltel proved impossible to achieve. As a result, he eventually lost Alltel's support.

Initially, the analyst community questioned Alltel's acquisition of a data processing services company. They considered it non-synergistic, not aligned with our core telecommunications business. After much discussion and rationalization, we successfully made the case that, not only might these two dissimilar organizations fit together, their alignment was visionary. The telecommunications and information-technology industries were beginning to merge functionality, and it became clear that networks and computing were interdependent. However, the truth is that Alltel was a rural telephone company, a capital-intensive utility led in a patriarchal style. Systematics was a mid-size, banking-oriented software company focused on a dying banking market, with a large number of technical employees, and led in an egalitarian manner, typical of software companies. The cultural and financial differences in these two organizations proved too great to ever merge them. A few years of mediocre performance completed Alltel's disenchantment. Systematics' acquisition and divestiture was a successful financial transaction; but the management and strategic diversion of this start-and-stop expansion into information services never produced its intended business value.

> Long-term success in a merger or acquisition is all about the relationship, or the marriage, not the attraction. The big lesson here: Combining companies is difficult, particularly when both companies are attempting to maintain any unique characteristics. Any expectations that "business as usual" will prevail after a merger will likely be a fantasy. I have not been involved in any successful mergers, and the only successful acquisitions I have seen follow one of two patterns:
>
> 1. The acquiring company takes a "scorched earth" policy with the acquired company's strategy, culture and management. In other words, the acquirer aggressively and quickly gets rid of it all and replaces it with the acquirer's.
>
> 2. The acquirer treats the newly possessed company as a financial transaction, heavily incents the acquired management to meet certain targets, and then leaves them alone.

Unfortunately for my long-term co-workers and me, when Alltel became disenchanted with Systematics, that applied to all Systematics' executives. The first bunch to go, with Alltel's encouragement, included the CEO and his cronies. The incoming CEO was a young investment banker closely connected to both Alltel's and Stephens' senior management. He was financially astute with excellent merger/acquisition analytic and deal background, but had little experience as a leader or manager. In addition, he possessed an impersonal communication style that made him appear distant as a leader. That caused the remaining Systematics executive management to first ignore him, then resist, and finally give up in frustration. As a result, Systematics lost most of its strong leadership. The best people found other opportunities or were laid off. In the long run, the remaining management team never realized the goals or synergy Alltel expected, and the company was sold.

Here's another of my more significant career accomplishments, and a reason you should pay attention to this book: I survived all these changes! I'll have to admit a certain pleasure in seeing the imported group of IBMers go, but the time we spent fighting with each other brought no gains for our company. We were all losers because of it. In addition, these were all good people, and I liked them, particularly the CEOs. They were just put into extremely challenging roles and expected to accomplish nearly impossible results.

Eventually I also became disenchanted with the investment banker's leadership, and it appeared Alltel would leave him in place. As in a number of business circumstances, this guy was a good person, smart and well intentioned, with an assignment to generate some improvement. He was doing the best he could at the time. But I found him difficult to communicate with. I questioned his actions and motives because I never saw clearly what he was trying to accomplish. He would likely say the same about me, as we never established a sound basis for understanding. In most cases, that must develop through common experiences and trust. I began to believe he didn't value my efforts and contribution, which may have been an incorrect assumption on my part. But, all the same, that belief influenced my desire to leave.

Fortunately by that stage in my career, I could afford to exit if I chose. I toyed with the idea, but did not have a plan. What I needed was a push, something to move towards, rather than just something to leave. I don't think I'm unique in this behavior, but I have frequently needed some kind of outside influence to finalize a major personal decision. This might materialize as a simple confirmation statement from my spouse (e.g., "If you are going to buy a boat in a few years, why not buy it now?"), a family member or friend. More likely the push would come from my perception that I needed to act immediately, because the alternative was short-lived. That's how I had decided to join Alcoa and Systematics, and was also a factor in finally leaving Systematics.

In this case, the push came through an opportunity to join a small, Little Rock-based engineering services company that I considered another "Systematics" in the making. This local business was led by a young (under 40) entrepreneur/engineer with a significant amount of charisma. On a whim, I went to visit him. I found a $15 million business with plenty of work, filled with young technical employees, the type I had collaborated with at Systematics/Alltel.

We discussed the creation of a role for me as chief operations officer (the company didn't use titles, but that was the role). With only a minor amount of encouragement, I left Alltel and made the change.

This was a great example of wanting something to be true without examining the reality. While I've never looked back at leaving Alltel, this job change was probably not the proper move for me. That's not to say I didn't benefit from this experience. I learned much, both positive and negative, and I am a better leader and mentor today because of it.

In my pre-employment compensation discussions, the firm's exec committed to place some initial stock options in my package, but we never documented the details. This happened before I came to work, and I should have recognized it as a strong omen of future problems. I was basing my view of this company on what Systematics and Alltel had been. In addition, the CEO was a good communicator, and possessed an excellent understanding of information-technology employees and issues. This made him appear as a visionary leader in control.

Here's the lesson I learned: There is no excuse for a lack of due diligence in employment decisions. In this case, I'd have developed a more accurate view if I had talked to the investors and some customers. Also, I should have performed some investigative company research from sources outside the immediate references. I possibly could have found some conflicting opinions. That would have encouraged me to look harder before I made the job change. There are no guarantees I would have made a different decision with additional knowledge, but I wouldn't question my pre-employment analytic efforts as I do today.

As it turned out, this small business couldn't deliver on its promises—to customers, employees and investors. Breakdowns in all of these areas caused the company's eventual demise, and my participation couldn't prevent this from happening. Rapid growth without an executable plan did not generate sufficient return to satisfy the investors. I think I expected leadership that the CEO could not give. I'm sure he expected more from me than I contributed. I also found it much more difficult than I had expected to learn and adapt to a new service offering.

When it became apparent we could not survive or pay back our investors, the company chose an aggressive, close down strategy with negative consequences for suppliers, lenders and investors. Knowing I wouldn't have the stomach for this approach, and that I was too expensive to retain, the CEO asked me to leave. Given the circumstances, that was the correct decision. I appreciate his understanding and honesty in dealing with me. I left, having no association with the subsequent negative activity.

At age 53, I found myself with sufficient assets to live well and not work, though I was by no means wealthy under today's standards. In talking to a few friends in similar circumstances, I received consistent advice to develop a working routine, even if I chose not to work for a company. After some searching, I decided to lease an office, using it as a base to look for investment opportunities and do some consulting. I would consult enough to pay for the office, so this "playing around at work" would not be a cash drain. In today's market, the most significant problem with retiring early is seeing my friends and peers continue to work. In addition, I began to realize that I receive much personal satisfaction and energy from daily interaction with other people. These interpersonal relationships are a natural byproduct of work.

Many people find it difficult to transition from working into retirement, particularly when that change is sudden. It's best to do this gradually, by "tapering off" rather than just stopping. Many of my early baby boomer co-workers and peers look at ending their working careers in this slower manner. The ideal job allows us to maintain our business relationships, remain intellectually challenged, continue to learn, and work three days a week! Needless to say, it's a hard job to find. But it's worthwhile to realize this value and search for a career that will eventually allow you to taper off.

I accomplished the office-funding goal through consulting on information-technology expenditures. It was almost too easy finding investment opportunities to review.

> Regarding investing, many people have business plans and ideas, but no money. They would love to help you part with your money. I came to realize why most of these people are looking: Their plans and ideas are not good investments. I believe we've proven beyond doubt that capitalism is an ideal system, and civilizations can prosper when guided by its basic economic principles. However, just because capitalism works does not mean it's easy, or even fair. It's very difficult to match the needs of investors and entrepreneurs. Most business conflict occurs around the differing interests of a capitalistic society's principals—investors, management, customers, and employees.

I came close to working out a deal through a local venture-capital fund. At the last minute, the deal fell through because the current owners had difficulty giving up control. While I found this lost opportunity disappointing, I did become convinced that I was ready and willing to go back to work.

The opportunity to follow through came quickly: a call from a former Systematics co-worker who had joined Acxiom Corporation—THE other large, central Arkansas-based technology company. It had gained a reputation as an excellent place to work. As personnel began to leave Systematics, both voluntary and involuntary in the wake of the Alltel acquisition, many found a home at Acxiom.

I met a number of former business associates there, all of whom strongly encouraged me to come to work. Some consistent belief existed among them that Acxiom needed a few "old heads" to support the leadership structure as the company continued to grow. I met with the sales and operational leaders. They offered to put me to work under little structure, learn as much as I could, and they would help me find a place.

I found it difficult to learn Acxiom's business. But the environment proved positive, similar to the old Systematics with a genuine concern for and appreciation of employees. After a year, I moved into a senior leadership position, Group Leader, in Acxiom language. In this role, I led a dedicated team serving a few large clients in the credit-card industry. I found it an ideal position for that stage of business life, 30 years into my career. I was no longer a top executive, but could work with and influence Acxiom's executive team as much as I chose. They would listen to me, which was an honor. Sometimes they would even act on my opinions. In addition, I maintained an intense operational pace, working with capable and challenging employees, as well as customers important to the company. I didn't realize it at the time, but I was beginning to wind down my career. I was developing a working style and level that satisfied me. It also produced value for my company.

After five years at Acxiom and as I approached age 60, I began to tire of the pace. I could literally "feel" an increasing level of frustration at the repetitive nature of business problems. On a recurring basis we would deal with cost control issues, frequent organizational changes (not always effective), communication problems, short-term decisions for financial necessity versus long-term opportunities for stability, the need to improve sales versus the requirement to deliver quality, and many other natural and normal conflicts that occur when running a business. A number of years earlier, these problems had challenged me. Now I began to react negatively to normal levels of operational difficulty. I could tell I was starting to respond as if these issues were personal. They were not; they were just business.

Fortunately, my increasing personal frustration paralleled the development of this book. I also began to engage effectively in advising and counseling individuals at all levels of our company. I could see the value of my own personal experience related to their current issues and problems. For me, the thrill I received from helping co-workers navigate normal company issues opened the door for my career's next phase.

I intend to keep working as long as I am able, but my focus has clearly changed from improving companies to improving companies' employees. I will tap the energy I generate from working with others, leveraging it to benefit as many people as possible. I'll do it through using this book and direct involvement in management training. I see this as a natural and normal career evolution. I am applying expertise, continuing to learn, and deriving personal satisfaction by working to help others.

> This is enough for me. I can work hard, emphasize doing the right thing, and have fun doing it. You can do the same!

Index